How to access the supplemental online resource

We are pleased to provide access to an online resource that supplements *Everyone Can!: Skill Development and Assessment in Elementary Physical Education*. This resource offers over 2,000 pages of teaching materials to design, implement, and evaluate a physical education program. It includes assessment-based instructional activities, games, station cards, posters, score sheets, and accommodations for individuals with disabilities, all designed to ensure both teacher and student success. We are certain you will enjoy this comprehensive set of teaching materials.

Accessing the online resource is easy! Follow these steps if you purchased a new book:

1. Using your web browser, go to **www.HumanKinetics.com/ EveryoneCan**.

2. Click on the **View Online Resource** button.

3. Click on the please register now link. You will create your personal profile and password at this time.

4. Write your e-mail and password down for future reference. Keep it in a safe place. You'll use this e-mail address and password to access your profile any subsequent time you visit the Human Kinetics Web site. Logging into this profile will grant you access to the online resource.

5. Once you are registered, enter the key code exactly as it is printed at the right, including all hyphens. Click **Submit**

6. Once the key code has been submitted, you will see a welcome screen. Click the **Continue** button to open your online resource.

7. After you enter the key code the first time, you will not need to use it again to access the online resource. In the future, simply log in using your e-mail and the password you created.

How to access the online resource if you purchased a used book:

You may purchase access to the online resource by visiting **www.HumanKinetics.com/EveryoneCan** or by calling 1-800-747-4457 in the U.S.; 1-800-465-7301 in Canada; +44 (0) 113 255 5665 in Europe; 08 8372 0999 in Australia; or 0800 222 062 in New Zealand.

For technical support, send an e-mail to:
support@hkusa.com . . . . U.S. and international customers
info@hkcanada.com . . . . Canadian customers
academic@hkeurope.com . . . . European customers
keycodesupport@hkaustralia.com . . . . Australian customers

HUMAN KINETICS
The Information Leader in Physical Activity

D/A: 02-09

MW00560274

Product: Everyone Can!: Skill Development and Asses in Elementary Physical Education online re

Key code: KELLY-3JYTR3JZ-9780736095587

This unique code allows you access to the online resource.

Access is provided if you have purchased a new book.
Once submitted, the code may not be entered for any other user.

HUMAN KINETICS ONLINE RESOURCE

EVERYONE CAN!

Skill Development and Assessment in Elementary Physical Education

Luke E. Kelly

Janet A. Wessel

Gail M. Dummer

Thomas Sampson

Human Kinetics

Library of Congress Cataloging-in-Publication Data

Kelly, Luke.
  Everyone can! : skill development and assessment in elementary
physical education / Luke Kelly ... [et al.].
     p. cm.
  ISBN-13: 978-0-7360-6212-1 (soft cover : alk. paper)
  ISBN-10: 0-7360-6212-2 (soft cover : alk. paper)
  1. Physical education for children with disabilities. 2.
Ability--Testing. I. Title.
  GV445.K35 2009
  372.86--dc22

                                   2009020455

ISBN-10: 0-7360-6212-2 (print)
ISBN-13: 978-0-7360-6212-1 (print)

Copyright © 2010 by Luke Kelly, Janet Wessel, Gail Dummer, and Thomas Sampson

The Web addresses cited in this text were current as of November 2009, unless otherwise noted.

Acquisitions Editor: Scott Wikgren
Developmental Editor: Bethany J. Bentley
Assistant Editors: Anne Rumery and Elizabeth Evans
Copyeditor: John Wentworth
Permission Manager: Dalene Reeder
Graphic Designer: Fred Starbird
Graphic Artist: Dawn Sills
Cover Designer: Bob Reuther
Photograph (cover): © Human Kinetics
Art Manager: Kelly Hendren
Associate Art Manager: Alan L. Wilborn
Illustrator: Tammy Page
Printer: Versa Press

Printed in the United States of America   10 9 8 7 6 5 4 3 2 1

The paper in this book is certified under a sustainable forestry program.

Human Kinetics
Web site: www.HumanKinetics.com

United States: Human Kinetics
P.O. Box 5076
Champaign, IL 61825-5076
800-747-4457
e-mail: humank@hkusa.com

Canada: Human Kinetics
475 Devonshire Road Unit 100
Windsor, ON N8Y 2L5
800-465-7301 (in Canada only)
e-mail: info@hkcanada.com

Europe: Human Kinetics
107 Bradford Road
Stanningley
Leeds LS28 6AT, United Kingdom
+44 (0) 113 255 5665
e-mail: hk@hkeurope.com

Australia: Human Kinetics
57A Price Avenue
Lower Mitcham, South Australia 5062
08 8372 0999
e-mail: info@hkaustralia.com

New Zealand: Human Kinetics
P.O. Box 80
Torrens Park, South Australia 5062
0800 222 062
e-mail: info@hknewzealand.com

E3583

Contents

PART I

EVERYONE CAN!
ACHIEVEMENT-BASED CURRICULUM (ABC)

PART II

EVERYONE CAN!
ONLINE RESOURCES

Preface

Over the past 30 years our nation's education system has been responding to unprecedented demands to reach higher rates of achievement for all students and to serve an increasingly diverse student body. To address these issues, a number of educational reforms have been initiated to make our education system more standards-based and accountable. These recent reforms were initiated by the 1983 report by the National Commission on Excellence in Education, *A Nation at Risk*, and are currently reflected in the passage and implementation of the No Child Left Behind (NCLB) Act of 2002. Two major implications of this act have been the establishment of state performance standards for student achievement required for schools' accreditation and mandatory assessment plans to evaluate the achievement of these standards. While physical education was not directly addressed in NCLB, the implications are clear. As time and resources allow, states and schools will need to implement assessment programs to evaluate the degree to which students are achieving established standards in all content areas, including physical education.

With regard to the changing diversity of the student population, two significant changes have developed with implications for physical education. First, the passage of Public Law 94-142, the Education of All Handicapped Children Act (EHA) in 1975 guaranteed all school-aged children, regardless of disability, the right to a free and appropriate public education. This law, now known as IDEA (Individuals with Disabilities Education Act), has led to the inclusion of the majority of students with disabilities into the general education curriculum, including physical education. To illustrate the impact of this legislation, it is estimated that there are approximately 6 million school-aged children in the United States. This translates to 3 or 4 students with disabilities being included in an average physical education class of 30 students. The impact of inclusion of students with disabilities is that we need to prepare teachers with the skills to address

a wider range of abilities in their classes as well as to accommodate a greater variety of learning styles. The second change influencing physical education is the change in physical activity levels and the increased levels of obesity and related health risks (e.g., hypertension, high cholesterol, Type 2 diabetes, coronary heart disease, stroke, gallbladder disease, osteoarthritis, respiratory problems, and cancer) occurring in school-aged students. For example, the latest CDC information (CDC, 2007) on obesity shows that the prevalence of overweight children has increased from 1980 to 2004 from 5.0 to 13.9 percent for students aged 6 through 11 years old and from 6.5 to 18.8 percent for students aged 12 through 19 years old. In addition, CDC data (CDC, 2003) shows that "61.5% of children aged 9 through 13 years do not participate in any organized physical activity during their non-school hours and that 22.6% do not engage in any free-time physical activity." These data suggest that in an average elementary class of 30 students, approximately 6 students are overweight and 18 are not participating in any organized or free time physical activity outside of school.

So what is the connection between *Everyone Can* and these trends? *Everyone Can* is the integration of the Achievement-Based Curriculum (ABC) model (Kelly and Melograno, 2004) and over 40 years of research and development in creating physical education resource materials designed to help teachers address the physical and motor needs of their students. *Everyone Can's* roots are from the I CAN project directed by Janet Wessel and the staff of the Field Service Unit at Michigan State University. I CAN was initially designed to assist teachers at state residential institutions and special schools that address the physical education needs of their students with mental retardation. The development and field testing of I CAN was supported by several grants funded by the U.S. Department of Education–Special Education and Rehabilitative Service, formally called the Department of Health, Education, and Welfare–Bureau of Education for the Handicapped. With the passage of PL 94-142, I CAN was adapted and modified to address the physical education needs of students with disabilities in the least restrictive environment in public schools. Over the years, the I CAN materials have been adapted and modified and used as the foundation for many school physical education programs, state physical education standards (e.g., Michigan's Education and Assessment Program for Physical Education), and for standardized assessment instruments (e.g., Test of Gross Motor Development, Ulrich, 2000). The ABC model evolved out of I CAN's project work with schools through a series of grants funded by the U.S. Department of Education–National Diffusion Network. The ABC model is a decision-making process designed to systematically guide teachers through curriculum planning, student assessment, implement planning, teaching, and evaluation of their students and physical education instructional programs based on local, state, and national standards.

Everyone Can is the application of the ABC model to address the demand for accountable standards-based physical education programs and to provide assessment-based instructional resource materials to address the needs of today's inclusive elementary physical education classes. *Everyone Can* provides step-by-step procedures to guide schools and teachers through the processes of designing their curriculum, assessing, implementation planning, teaching, and

evaluation. In addition, *Everyone Can* provides extensive field-tested instruction materials to assist teachers in addressing the unique needs of the full range of students in their classes. The strength of *Everyone Can* is that it provides concrete examples to illustrate each of the steps in the ABC model, but it does not dictate what content should be taught or how it should be taught. Instead, the program guides teachers through a series of decisions that allows them to decide what content to include in their program and how to teach it. *Everyone Can* then provides a wealth of resources to assist them in implementing what they have designed.

Given the rising health risks associated with obesity in children and the growing need for all children to be more physically active, the need for high-quality physical education programs that can document that they are effective and achieving their stated goals has never been greater. *Everyone Can* has been designed to assist you and your fellow teachers in addressing these needs in your school district. We encourage you to take the first step and review the ABC process and the *Everyone Can* resources. Share and discuss these materials with your colleagues and then work collaboratively to develop an action plan to address your school district's physical education needs so that all students leave the program demonstrating mastery of the established local, state, and national standards.

Acknowledgments

The *Everyone Can* book and online resource is the culmination of several years of work and the imagination, support, and assistance of many individuals. This has been an exciting adventure and learning experience for all who have been involved. To everyone who contributed, we wish to express our admiration for your dedicated work as educators for helping to make this project a reality for all the children in physical education programs in our schools. We take this opportunity to acknowledge the generous contributions of our colleagues, committed elementary physical educators, graduate students, and our many friends who worked closely with us in creating the *Everyone Can* online instructional resources:

Jill Hough, physical education teacher in Okemos Public Schools, Okemos, Michigan

Emily J. Dummer, student in Cleveland Public Schools, Cleveland, Minnesota

Tom Moran, assistant professor at George Mason University in Harrisonburg, Virginia

Colton Moreno, student in East Lansing Public Schools

All the adapted physical education graduate students from 2005 to 2008 at the University of Virginia at Charlottesville

Dixie L. Durr, PhD, professor in the department of theater at Michigan State University

Students in the department of kinesiology at Michigan State University:

Melissa G.F. Alexander	Erin L. Hess
Lindsay M. Calhoon	Alison Knopic
Kelly R. Clor	Susan J. Miller
Michael P. DiCenzo	Katherine E. Schaeffer
Mark A. Dziak	Steve D. Sherer
	Joshua J. Smith
	Kara J. Stout

Michael J. Roskamp	Gerhild Ullmann
Theresa Pusateri	Lucas A. VanEtten

Aaron Moffett, PhD, assistant professor in the department of kinesiology at California State University at San Bernardino

Students in the department of kinesiology at California State University at San Bernardino:

Melissa Bender	Louie Mares
Jamaal Cannon	Monique Nolan
Pasqual Chavez	Guillermo Perezchica
Adriana A. Escobedo	Ryan Pacheco
Jennifer Gormley	Bethel Trice
	Ruth A. Wiley
Debra Howard	Jong Won Park
Paul Janeway	

Lauriece Zittel, PhD, associate professor in the department of kinesiology and physical education at Northern Illinois University

All the students in the department of kinesiology and physical education at Northern Illinois University:

Pamela Delnagro	Marc Gorecki
Kieran Fitzgerald	Tara McCarthy
	Joseph A. Ryback

We would also like to thank Scott Wikgren, acquisitions editor at Human Kinetics, for his willingness to support and follow through on this innovative and challenging project. In spite of a number of personal and technical challenges, Scott worked with us to make this project a reality. We would also like to thank Bethany Bentley, developmental editor, for the effort and time she devoted to this project. We greatly appreciate her organization, timeliness, and attention to detail, which facilitated the editing process and kept this project on schedule.

How to Use This Book and Online Resource

What you have in your hands is the most comprehensive and extensive set of elementary physical education teaching materials currently available in a single resource. Although primarily designed to be used as a preservice textbook in physical education teacher preparation programs, this book was also written with the needs of in-service teachers in mind. The uniqueness of this book is that it provides you with both the What and the How for teaching elementary physical education. The What is addressed by the Achievement-Based Curriculum (ABC) process in part I, and the How is addressed by the *Everyone Can* resource materials in part II. The ABC process is labeled the ABC success cycle in figure I.1 because it defines what decisions teachers

must make to design, implement, and evaluate a physical education program that ensures both teacher and student success—effective instruction that results in *all* students mastering the content in the curriculum.

The ABC success cycle is made up of five components. Although shown as discrete components in the illustration it is important to understand that they are interdependent and thus must all be addressed to have a successful physical education program. Program planning is the first component and involves creating a functional physical education curriculum that clearly communicates the program content, when it is taught, and when it is expected to be achieved by the students. The second component is assessment, which guides

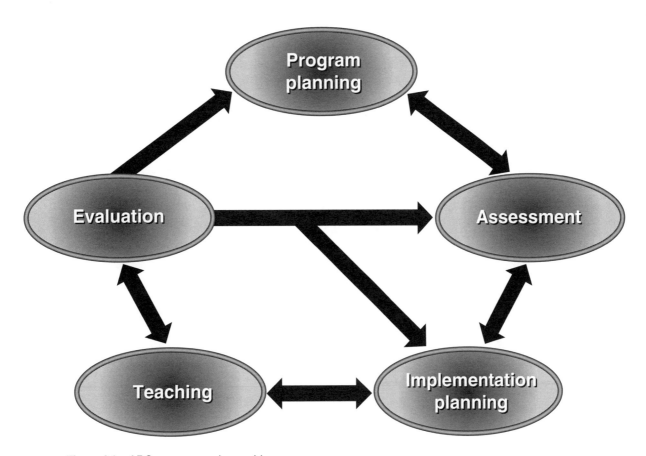

Figure I.1 ABC success cycle graphic.

teachers through the process of observing student performance on the content identified for instruction and identifying their current level of performance. With student assessment data in hand, teachers use this information to plan their instruction, which is called implementation planning, the third component. The fourth component is teaching, which involves managing the learning environment and implementing instruction so that students learn the content targeted for instruction. Finally, the last component is evaluation, which involves analyzing student reassessment data to maximize student achievement and program effectiveness.

Two of the more time challenging tasks involved in using the ABC model are developing a program plan and then defining the objectives (i.e., the content to be taught) as criterion-referenced assessment items that can be used to evaluate student performance and guide the planning of instruction. To facilitate the use of the ABC process and the *Everyone Can* resources, these two elements have been provided in the form of a model K-5 elementary physical educa-

tion curriculum (chapter 6). These two elements in turn are the keys to using the *Everyone Can* resources, which are described in detail in chapter 7. The mouse icon that can be found in the margin denotes an online resource. The program plan indicates what content should be taught and mastered at each grade level. The criterion-referenced assessment items break each objective down into small components, called focal points, which allow you to determine what each student needs to learn next on each objective. Once you know what objective and focal points your students need to work on, you are ready to tap into the *Everyone Can* online resources outlined in table I.1.

A quick review of table I.1 reveals that the online resource materials, located at www.HumanKinetics.com/EveryoneCan, are organized on two levels. The assessments, assessing activities, accommodations for individuals with disabilities, scoresheets, and posters are designed around the objectives with one of each of these resources provided for each of the 70 objectives in the model K-5 program—for a total of 350

Table I.1 Overview of the *Everyone Can* Online Resource Materials

Everyone Can resource materials:	#	Resource description
Objective assessment items	70	Task analysis of objectives into skill levels and focal points to form criterion-referenced assessment items for the 70 most commonly taught objectives in K-5 physical education.
Assessing activities	70	Suggested games and activities that a class of students can be engaged in so the teacher can observe and assess their students on each objective.
Accommodations	70	Guidelines on how teachers can modify each performance objective and instruction to address the unique needs of students with disabilities.
Scoresheets	140	Forms that allow teachers to record students' performances of skill levels and focal points of each objective.
Posters	70	Pictures of the key focal points of each objective.
Teaching instructional activities	1,026	Detailed instruction recommendations on how to teach each skill level and focal point of each objective.
Station task cards	1,026	These cards are instructional aids to be used by teachers to define instruction stations in their classes designed to focus on focal points of each performance objective.
Games	313	Large- and small-group games are provided for each performance objective and keyed to each focal point of each performance objective.

resources at the objective level. The remaining instructional resources are organized around the focal points and skill levels within each objective. These include instruction activities for the teacher, station cards, and games—in all, there are more than 2,000 instructional resources at the focal point and skill levels.

Now that you know the depth and breadth of the online resource materials provided with this book, you might be tempted to skip the reading and jump right onto the Internet. Although it is true that all resources can be used independently, the power of this package is that all materials are designed around the ABC process. To maximize your ability to meet your students' needs, we highly recommend that you read the first part of the book. The five chapters on the ABC process are presented in a condensed, easy-to-read, step-by-step process. Practical activities are provided at the end of each of these chapters to assist you in translating the concepts into practice. In addition, chapters 3 and 7 specifically address how to use the instruction materials in the online resource. Figure I.2 illustrates the relations among the chapters in the book and the *Everyone Can* resources. Content presented in the book chapters is denoted by clear rectangles, whereas the resources on the Web site are indicated by shaded rectangles with rounded corners.

Finally, chapter 8 addresses how to modify the model program plan and the instructional resources to meet your school's unique needs. It is important to understand that the ABC success cycle guides teachers through a decision-making process in which they decide what content should be in their program, when it should be taught and mastered, and how it should best be taught. Guidelines are also provided to assist teachers in using the ABC process to develop IEPs for their students with disabilities and for assisting parents who are homeschooling their children. The model program plan presented in chapter 6 and the *Everyone Can* teaching resources are provided as examples to help teachers get started using the ABC process. We understand that each teaching situation is unique and that many teachers face significant challenges, such as large class sizes, inadequate facilities and equipment, and limited amounts of instruction time. We strongly encourage teachers to experiment with the ABC process and the *Everyone Can* teaching materials, adapt them to their needs, and make them their own. Recommendations are provided in chapter 8 on how the ABC model and *Everyone Can* online resources can also be used to design a comprehensive physical education in-service program. Our goal is not to try and make everyone teach the same content or the same way but to assist teachers in providing the best physical education program they can.

Let the adventure begin. Nothing is more exciting than giving students new abilities, particularly for skills they have tried to learn and have been unsuccessful in mastering. With the ABC success cycle and the *Everyone Can* online teaching resources, you now have the knowledge and tools to teach your students all the physical and motor skills they need to live active and healthy lives.

ABC Model

Everyone Can Resources

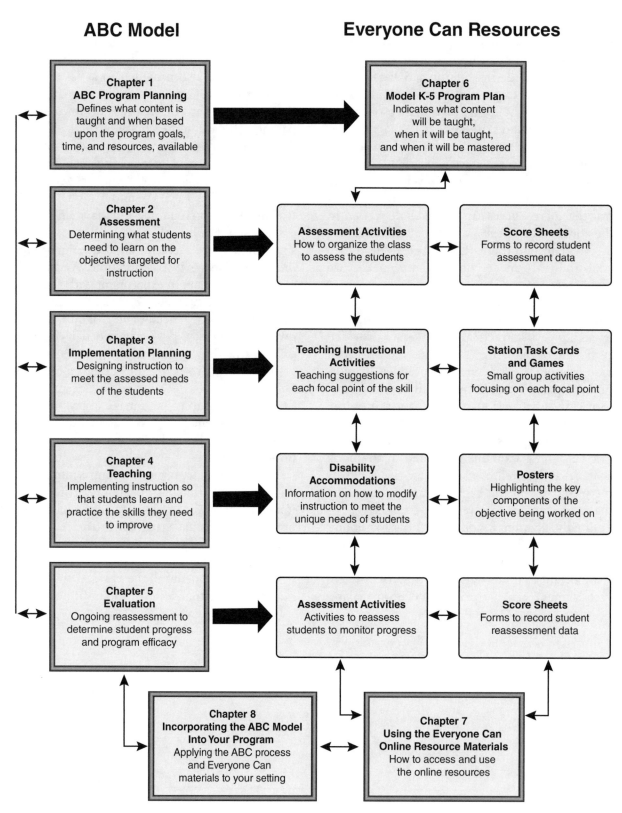

Figure I.2 Chapter by resource graphic.

PART I

EVERYONE CAN!

ACHIEVEMENT-BASED CURRICULUM (ABC)

CHAPTER 1

ABC PROGRAM PLANNING

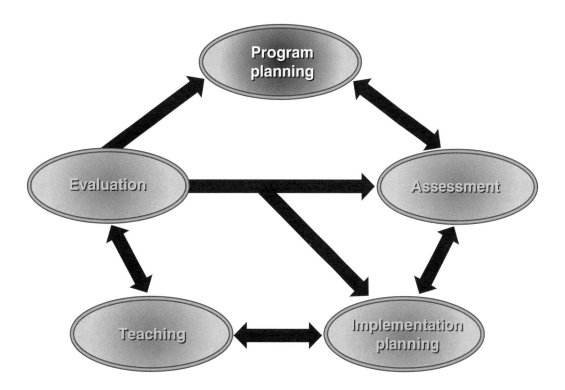

The *Everyone Can* instructional materials presented in this book and the accompanying online resource represent the most comprehensive and extensive elementary physical education materials available in a single resource. To optimally use these materials to maximize student achievement in physical education and teacher effectiveness you must first understand the underlying organizational structure. For the *Everyone Can* materials this structure is the Achievement-Based Curriculum (ABC) model (Kelly & Melograno, 2004). The ABC model is composed of five integrated components: Program planning, Assessment, Implementation planning, Teaching, and Evaluation. Each of these components is introduced in this text in a separate chapter to provide teachers with a basic foundation for effectively using the *Everyone Can* materials.

This first chapter introduces ABC program planning. After reading this chapter, you should be able to . . .

1. Name the steps involved in creating an ABC program plan.

2. Explain the purpose of the program philosophy, program goals, and objectives in the ABC program planning process.

3. Describe the relations among program goal emphasis, average objective mastery time, and instructional time in program planning.

4. Explain how to develop yearly program plans and sequential instructional blocks across time for the school year by grade.

5. Explain why program and block planning are fundamental for successful implementation of the ABC model of instruction.

6. Explain the importance of objective assessment items in the implementation of the ABC model of instruction and how they are defined.

Ever wonder how teachers determine how much content can be taught in their physical education program or how the content should be sequenced so that students can learn more advanced skills? These are the types of questions addressed in ABC program planning. The ABC program plan communicates to students, parents, and administrators the answers to these questions:

- What content is being taught in physical education?
- Why is this content being taught?
- Where are the students on the content being taught?
- What needs to be learned by each student?
- What has been learned by each student as a result of instruction?

In this chapter we'll review the basic steps in the program planning process and provide concrete examples of each step.

The materials developed by these procedures and prescribed in this chapter are adaptations of an ABC planning process presented by Kelly and Melograno (2004) in *Developing the Physical Education Curriculum: An Achievement-Based Approach*. A model plan is illustrated in this chapter, and the entire process is presented in chapter 6. Seven

Program Planning Steps

1. Establish a program philosophy, goals, and objectives.

2. Assign program goal emphasis.

3. Determine instructional time and average objective mastery time.

4. Calculate the total number of objectives per goal.

5. Finalize program scope and sequence.

6. Create yearly teaching learning maps.

7. Identify objective assessment items and create scoresheets.

basic tenets underlie the development of an ABC physical education curriculum:

1. It is a cooperative venture using input from all constituencies and is integrated within the overall school curriculum.

2. It is designed from the top down based on resources available and then implemented from the bottom up according to the developmental level of the students.

3. It aligns the school's goals with established national and state standards for physical education.

4. It coordinates the efforts of the physical education faculty so the same goals and respective objectives are worked on at the same program levels in each school and so all students achieve the objectives defined in the program.

5. It provides a means by which the effectiveness in reaching the stated goals and objectives of the curriculum of the program can be documented.

6. It ensures that the physical and motor needs of all children in the program are being addressed.

7. It provides a method for ongoing evaluation and in-service training to improve the quality of the program and teaching.

The ABC plan serves as a case study for readers to understand their importance in instructional planning and teaching. Each ABC physical education plan is designed around the unique needs and characteristics of a particular school. For example, the model plan presented in this text is based on students receiving daily physical education five times a week. If you have physical education only twice a week, you will not be able to include as many objectives in your curriculum. In this case the ABC plan presented here should be viewed as a model example and not as the perfect or definitive plan for elementary physical education. The

steps described in this chapter are summaries of the procedures involved in the development of an elementary physical education curriculum.

STEP ❶
ESTABLISH A PROGRAM PHILOSOPHY, GOALS, AND OBJECTIVES

The first step in the planning process involves the establishment of a program philosophy, program goals, and objectives for each goal. The *program philosophy* is a statement of the underlying values and intended benefits to be gained from participation in the program. These values and benefits are further defined in the form of *program goals* that define the outcomes that should be achieved through the delivery of the instructional program. Most schools use existing standards such as the NASPE standards and their state physical education standards as starting points and then customize them to match the needs of their district. Table 1.1 shows the relations among the NASPE standards and the program goals of the model K-5 program plan presented in chapter 6.

Program objectives define the essential program content to be taught and ultimately achieved by the students to meet the program goals. For example, a program goal might be for students to leave the program with the fundamental object control skills they need to learn and participate in a variety of games and sports; in this case, the program objectives might be for each student to

Table 1.1   Relations Among NASPE Standards and Program Goals

NASPE standards for physical education	Model K-5 elementary physical education program goals	Sample objectives
Standard 1: Demonstrates competency in motor skills and movement patterns needed to perform a variety of physical activities.	1. Students will leave the program with awareness of their bodies and how their bodies interact in space and in activity.	Body awareness: body parts, body actions
Standard 2: Demonstrates understanding of movement concepts, principles, strategies, and tactics as they apply to the learning and performance of physical activities.	2. Students will leave the program with the personal and social skills needed to successfully participate in physical education and group games and sports.	Personal/social: work habits, social skills

(continued)

Table 1.1 *(continued)*

NASPE standards for physical education	Model K-5 elementary physical education program goals	Sample objectives
Standard 3: Participates regularly in physical activity.	3. Students will leave the program with the locomotor (e.g., run, hop) skills needed to participate in a variety of societal games, sports, and fitness activities.	Locomotor skills: run, hop
Standard 4: Achieves and maintains a health-enhancing level of physical fitness.	4. Students will leave the program with the basic dance and rhythm skills needed to participate in and learn common societal dances.	Rhythm and dance: move to even beat, Polka
Standard 5: Exhibits responsible personal and social behavior that respects self and others in physical activity settings.	5. Students will leave the program with fundamental body control skills needed to manage their bodies in different orientations and movements.	Body control: forward roll, cartwheel
Standard 6: Values physical activity for health, enjoyment, challenge, self-expression, and/or social interaction.	6. Students will leave the program with the physical fitness knowledge and skills needed to develop, maintain, and manage their fitness by participating in daily moderate and vigorous activity	Physical fitness: push-ups, stretching
	7. Students will leave the program with the fundamental object control skills (e.g., throw, catch) needed to learn and participate in a wide variety of our societal games and sports.	Object control skills: overhand throw, catch

master the underhand roll, overhand throw, catch, and kick. Figure 1.1 shows the *Everyone Can* objective for catching. The uniqueness of the *Everyone Can* materials is that every program objective has been defined as a criterion-referenced assessment item. These Objective Assessment Items (OAIs) define each objective in terms of skill levels and the related critical elements (called focal points) that must be mastered by the students. In figure 1.1 you see that the catch OAI has three skill levels. The first skill level defines the mature pattern. To achieve this level, the student must successfully demonstrate all the performance criteria labeled as focal points a through g. Focal points are the critical performance criteria that must be demonstrated on two out of three trials to demonstrate mastery. Once students achieve skill level 1 of an objective, they then progress to skill levels 2 and 3.

To complete step 1, a curriculum committee is typically created with representatives from the community, school administration, physical education staff, students, and other teaching staff. This committee then develops a physical education program philosophy statement that typically ends with a set of goals (see figure 1.2). Next a list of potential objectives are identified and ranked for each goal. Note that the elementary physical education goals are based on the skills students need to learn team sport and lifetime sport skills to be taught at the middle and secondary levels.

Table 1.2 (p. 8) shows the rank-ordered lists of objectives for the first program goal in the model elementary physical education program being used as an example in this chapter. Note under the goal statement the list of objectives with each objective being assigned a rank. The rank indicates the relative importance of each objective.

Teachers are asked to rank the objectives under each goal by responding to this question: If only one objective could be taught under this goal, what objective would you teach? This process is repeated (if only two objectives could be taught, etc.), and the result is a rank-ordered list of objectives for each goal. Table 1.3 (p. 8) shows the rank-ordered lists of objectives for all of the goals in the model program.

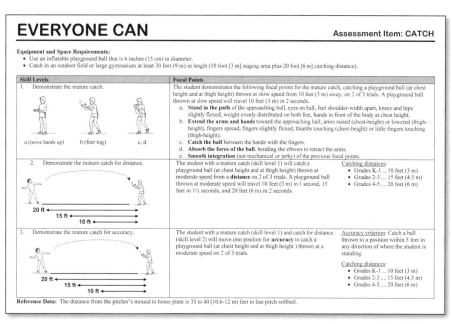

Figure 1.1 *Everyone Can* objective assessment item for the catch.

Illustrations reprinted from J. Wessel, 1976, *I can: Object control* (North Brook, IL: Hubbard Scientific Company), 89. By permission of J. Wessel.

FIGURE 1.2
Sample Philosophy Statement

HIGHLAND ELEMENTARY PHYSICAL EDUCATION

Physical education in the Highland School District is an integral part of the overall school curriculum and an essential part of the development of all students. The community and faculty agree that students need physical education so they can be physically active, which is essential to the development and maintenance of health and fitness. It is believed that physical education provides students with the fundamental motor skills and knowledge needed to learn and participate in our societal games and sports. It is important that students not only experience these skills in physical education but that they also master a level of proficiency that affords them the ability to participate in a variety of physical recreational sports and activities both during and after their school years. To achieve these ends, the Highland School District is committed to providing daily physical education to all elementary students to be delivered by certified physical education specialists. The Highland School District also commits to providing the physical education program with

appropriate facilities and resources needed to implement the program. The Highland Physical Education program is based on the National Association of Physical Education and Sport national physical education standards and is designed for students to achieve the following goals by the end of fifth grade:

1. Students will leave the program with awareness of their bodies and how their bodies interact in space and in activity.

2. Students will leave the program with the personal and social skills needed to successfully participate in physical education and group games and sports.

3. Students will leave the program with the locomotor (e.g., run, hop) skills needed to participate in a variety of societal games, sports, and fitness activities.

4. Students will leave the program with the basic dance and rhythm skills needed to participate in and learn common societal dances.

(continued)

Figure 1.2 *(continued)*

5. Students will leave the program with fundamental body control skills needed to manage their bodies in different orientations and movements.

6. Students will leave the program with the physical fitness knowledge and skills needed to develop, maintain, and manage

their fitness by participating in daily moderate and vigorous activity.

7. Students will leave the program with the fundamental object control skills (e.g., throw, catch) needed to learn and participate in a wide variety of our societal games and sports.

Table 1.2   Sample Program Goal With Rank-Ordered Objectives

Consensus Forming Worksheet

Goal Area: Body Awareness   Ranking Round: 3

Objectives	Teacher 1	Teacher 2	Teacher 3	Teacher 4	Teacher 5	Final
Body parts	1	3	1	1	1	1.4 (1)
Personal space	3	1	2	4	4	2.8 (2)
Directionality	8	9	3	6	9	7.0 (7)
Body actions	2	4	4	5	2	3.4 (3)
Directions in space	5	5	6	7	6	5.8 (6)
Spatial awareness	7	8	7	9	8	7.8 (8)
Body planes	6	6	8	2	5	5.4 (5)
General space	4	2	5	3	3	3.8 (4)
Balance	9	7	9	8	7	8.0 (9)

Table 1.3   Model Program Goals With Rank-Ordered Objectives

Goal area	Objectives	Final rank
Body awareness	Body parts	1
	Personal space	2
	Body actions	3
	General space	4
	Body planes	5
	Directions in space	6
	Directionality	7
	Spatial awareness	8
	Balance	9
Personal/social	Follow instructions	1
	Work habits	2

Goal area	Objectives	Final rank
	Self-respect	3
	Social skills	4
	Team play	5
	Self-advocacy	6
	Respect for equipment	7
	Cooperation	8
	Sportsmanship	9
Locomotor skills	Run	1
	Gallop	2
	Hop	3
	Slide	4
	Skip	5
	Leap	6
	Long jump	7
	Vertical jump	8
	Run backward	9
	Combination skills	10
Rhythm and dance	Even beat	1
	Uneven beat	2
	Accented beat	3
	Communication through movement	4
	Polka	5
	Schottische	6
	Square dance	7
	Line dance	8
	Creative dance	9
Body control	Log roll	1
	Shoulder roll	2
	Forward roll	3
	Backward roll	4
	Two-point balances	5
	One-point balances	6
	Rope jump	7
	Balance beam walk	8

(continued)

Table 1.3   *(continued)*

Goal area	Objectives	Final rank
	Cartwheel	9
	Headstand	10
	Handstand	11
	Kip-up	12
	Round-off	13
Physical fitness	Partial curl-ups	1
	Endurance run	2
	Push-ups	3
	V-sit reach	4
	BMI	5
	Stretching	6
	Warm-up	7
	Active lifestyle	8
	Cardiorespiratory exertion	9
	Speed	10
	Power	11
	Skinfolds	12
Object-control skills	Underhand roll	1
	Underhand throw	2
	Overhand throw	3
	Catch	4
	Fielding fly balls	5
	Fielding ground balls	6
	Two-arm sidearm strike	7
	Forehand strike	8
	Backhand strike	9
	Overhand strike	10
	Kick stationary ball	11
	Kick moving ball	12
	Trap ball	13
	Throw-in	14
	Foot dribble	15
	Two-handed chest pass	16
	Bounce pass	17

Goal area	Objectives	Final rank
	Hand dribble	18
	Set shot	19
	Forearm pass	20
	Overhand pass	21
	Underhand strike	22
	Frisbee throw	23
	Lay-up	24
	Punting	25
	Jump shot	26
	Rebounding	27
	Tennis volley	28

STEP ❷
ASSIGN PROGRAM GOAL EMPHASIS

Program goal emphasis is the percent of emphasis each program goal should receive across the grade levels in the program. This is an important step because all the goals are not equally important or appropriate at the various grades. For example, body awareness skills are more important at the lower levels and are prerequisites for learning many object control skills, which receive greater emphasis at the upper grade levels. Table 1.4

shows the seven goal areas identified for the model program. To determine the program goal emphasis, all the teachers of the program indicated what percent emphasis they felt each goal should receive across each grade level. These values were averaged, with final averages shown in table 1.4. Note the last column of the table shows the program emphasis for each goal. This value was calculated by summing the teachers' average values for each goal and then dividing by the number of grades (in this case 6). For example, the teachers indicated for their Personal/Social goal that on average they wanted to devote 10

Table 1.4 Program Goal Emphasis Chart

Goal area	K	1	2	3	4	5	Program emphasis
Body awareness	27	18	9				9.0%
Personal/social	10	10	7	7	7	7	8.0%
Locomotor	18	18	9	9	9	9	12.0%
Rhythm and dance	18	18	9	9			9.0%
Body control	9	27	18	18	18		15.0%
Health and fitness			12	21	21	30	14.0%
Object control	18	9	36	36	45	54	33.0%
Sum = 100%	100	100	100	100	100	100	100%

* Each value in the chart represents the teachers' average percent ratings.

percent of the program time during kindergarten and first grade and on average 7 percent of the instructional time for grades 2 through 5. These values were summed and then divided by 6 to get an overall program goal emphasis of 8 percent for this goal (48/6 = 8).

Note that the values in table 1.4 reflect the values and interests of one specific group of teachers who were developing this curriculum. The program goal emphasis values produced are thus unique for each group of teachers that goes through this process. The group of teachers in the current example had a strong emphasis on object control skills. Another group of teachers in another district might have a greater emphasis on dance or personal/social objectives. The important point is that you only have 100 percent to divide across the number of goals you decide to include in your program plan. The more emphasis you decide to put on any given goal, the less you are going to be able to put on the remaining goals.

STEP ❸
DETERMINE INSTRUCTIONAL TIME AND AVERAGE OBJECTIVE MASTERY TIME

This step of the planning process involves determining the total number of program objectives that can be taught and mastered in the amount of instructional time available for physical education. Table 1.5 shows the calculation of physical education *instructional time* per year. The model curriculum used in this book is based on physical

education being taught five times per week for 30 minutes each session. If physical education is offered less frequently in your school, the amount of available instructional time will be less for your program. Table 1.5 also indicates that the total amount of instructional time has been decreased by 10 percent to account for lost instructional time caused by teacher absences, assemblies, and other events that reduce the amount of instructional time in physical education each year.

To determine the number of program objectives that the students can work on in the available instructional time, teachers also estimate the *average objective mastery time*. It is important that all teachers are thinking of mastery in the same terms. In the model curriculum we are examining, average objective mastery time is defined as the amount of time needed to teach all the essential focal points of skill level 1 of each objective to a typical class of students. Take a moment to review the skill level 1 focal points of the catch in figure 1.1. These estimates also assume that students are developmentally ready to learn the skill but that most of them have no functional competency. Because some objectives in different goal areas require more or less time to teach, a process is used in which an estimate is made for a typical objective within each goal area, and then this estimate is weighted by the program goal emphasis calculated for each goal area. Note that these estimates are school dependent and affected by many local variables such as class size, number of students included with disabilities, teacher experience, and instructional facilities. Table 1.6 shows a worksheet used by a group of teachers to estimate their average objective mastery time.

Table 1.5 Instructional Time Calculation

#Classes per week	#Weeks per year	# Minutes per class	# Grades	Total minutes	Minus 10%	Minutes available	Minutes per year	Hours per year
1	36	30	6	6,480	-648	5,832	972	16.2
2	36	30	6	12,960	-1,296	11,664	1,944	32.4
3	36	30	6	19,440	-1,944	17,496	2,916	48.6
4	36	30	6	25,920	-2,592	23,328	3,888	64.8
5	36	30	6	32,400	-3,240	29,160	4,860	81.0

The first column in the table shows the seven program goals. In the second column a typical objective for this goal area has been selected. Each teacher then independently estimated how long it would take to teach a typical class mastery (as defined by the *Everyone Can* skill level 1 focal points) for each of the identified objectives. The last column on the right side of the table shows the teachers' average estimate (i.e., sum of the individual teacher's estimates divided by five—the number of teachers).

Now that there is an estimate of how long it takes to teach mastery of common objectives in each goal area, these estimates are weighted to reflect the program goal emphasis. This is done by multiplying the program goal emphasis values calculated in table 1.4 times the average objective mastery times calculated in table 1.6. These calculations are shown in table 1.7. The first column shows the seven program goals. The second column shows the average objective mastery times for each goal taken from table 1.6. The

Table 1.6 Average Objective Mastery Time By Goal

Category	Sample objective	Teacher ratings					
		1	2	3	4	5	Avg.
Body awareness	Body actions	120	400	300	360	420	320
Personal/ Social	Follow instructions	180	360	400	320	340	320
Locomotor	Skip	360	420	440	480	600	460
Rhythm and dance	Polka	360	380	340	400	420	380
Body control	Backward roll	360	460	440	360	380	400
Health and fitness	Partial curl-ups	500	600	640	420	440	520
Object control	Overhand throw	420	600	560	400	520	500

Table 1.7 Calculating Average Objective Mastery Time for the Program

Category	(a) Estimated average (from table 1.6)	(b) Program % goal emphasis (from table 1.4)	(c) Estimated time by goal weight (a) × (b)
Body awareness	320	9%	28.8
Personal/social	320	8%	25.6
Locomotor	460	12%	55.2
Rhythm and dance	380	9%	34.2
Body control	400	15%	60.0
Health and fitness	520	14%	72.8
Object control	500	33%	165.0
Sum	2900	100%	441.6

third column shows the program goal emphases from table 1.4. The second and third columns are then multiplied times each other to produce a weighted time estimate, which is shown in the last column. Finally, the weighted time estimates for each goal area shown in the last column are summed to produce the overall average objective mastery time for objectives in this program (i.e., 441.6 minutes).

The amount of content that can actually be taught in any given physical education program is a function of the amount of instruction time available and the time needed to teach mastery of each objective. Using the total amount of time calculated in table 1.5 for five days a week of 30 minutes of physical education divided by the average objective mastery time calculated in table 1.7 reveals that a total of 66 objectives can be taught in this model program (29,160 min/441.6 min = 66 objectives). This also means that 11 objectives should be mastered during each year of the program (66 objectives/6 years = 11 objectives per year).

STEP ❹
CALCULATE THE TOTAL NUMBER OF OBJECTIVES PER GOAL

Now that you know what emphasis each goal should receive across the program (table 1.4), how much time is available for instruction (table 1.5),

and how long it takes to teach an average objective (table 1.7), the number of objectives that can be included in the program for each goal can be calculated. Table 1.8 shows how these decisions are made. The first column of the table lists the seven program goals. The second column shows the average program goal emphasis calculated for each goal in step 2 and calculated in table 1.4. The third column indicates the total number of objectives that can be covered in the program. This value was calculated at the end of step 3. Finally, the last column shows the total number of objectives that can be included in the program for each goal. These values are calculated by multiplying the program goal emphasis times the total number of program objectives. For example, for the health and fitness goal the program goal emphasis was 14 percent. This value was multiplied times the total number of program objectives (66), resulting in a total of 9 objectives being included for this goal area (.14 × 66 = 9.24). Because you cannot teach fractions of objectives, the total number of objectives for each goal is rounded up or down to a whole number so that their sum equals the total number of objectives identified for the program.

It should be noted that the teachers in this example included five fitness objectives that parallel the items on the President's Council's Health Fitness Challenge (partial curl-ups, endurance run, push-ups, V-Sit reach, and BMI). We have included in the *Everyone Can* resource materials and objective assessment items additional fitness

Table 1.8   Calculating the Number of Objectives per Program Goal

Goal area	Program goal emphasis	Total number of program objectives	Number of objectives for this goal
Body awareness	9.0%	66	6
Personal/social	8.0%	66	5
Locomotor	12.0%	66	8
Rhythm and dance	9.0%	66	6
Body control	15.0%	66	10
Health and fitness	14.0%	66	9
Object control	33.0%	66	22
Total =	100.0%	66	66

objectives to support schools that may be using the traditional Presidential Physical Fitness test or other common fitness tests. If your school district uses another fitness test, you should review these items and adapt them as necessary to meet your needs. You will also have to adjust the norms used in skill levels 2 and 3 of these objectives.

STEP ❺
FINALIZE PROGRAM SCOPE AND SEQUENCE

Using the number of objectives identified for each goal in table 1.8, you now return to table 1.3 on page 8 and select the number of objectives based on the objective rankings. For example, nine objectives were initially identified and rank ordered for the body awareness goal area. We now know that there is only enough time in the program to include six of these objectives, so the first six objectives are selected based on their ranks (e.g., body parts, personal space, body actions, general space, body planes, and directions in space). Note that you will almost always have more content identified and ranked under each goal than you have time to teach. One of the primary benefits of using the ABC planning process is that it guides you through the difficult process of deciding how much and what content to include in your program based on your available resources. Without this process, teachers typically try to include too much content in their program plans. This results in trying to teach too

much content in too little time and students not achieving the target goals of the program.

Now that you know which objectives will be included in the program plan for each goal, the next step is to sequence these objectives across the six grades in the program (table 1.9). Remember that the objectives were ranked earlier in terms of their overall importance and not necessarily based on when they should be taught developmentally. The purpose of this step is to look at all of the objectives across the goals identified to be included in the program and then to developmentally sequence them so they are taught in the appropriate sequence and at the correct time. NASPE (2008) and many states have also established benchmarks at which students are expected to demonstrate established performance measures on selected objectives. These standards should also be reviewed and considered when sequencing the objectives in the program plan. Note that how an objective is defined affects the grade level at which it should be achieved. The size of the ball, the distance it is thrown from, and the number of focal points used to define a skill like catching, for example, would all affect at which grade level students would be expected to master this skill. If students were required only to catch a large playground ball thrown from a short distance by trapping the ball between their hands, arms, and chest, this could easily be a skill targeted for mastery in kindergarten. If the ball were smaller and thrown from a greater distance, and the students were expected to catch and control the ball with only their hands, the skill

Table 1.9 Sample Scope and Sequence Chart

Goal area	Objective	Grades					
		K	1	2	3	4	5
Body awareness	Body parts	**					
	Body actions	**					
	Body planes	--	**				
	General space	**					
	Directions in space	--	**				
	Personal space		--	**			

(continued)

Table 1.9 *(continued)*

Goal area	Objective	Grades					
		K	1	2	3	4	5
Personal/social	Follow instructions	**	R				
	Work habits	--	**	R			
	Self-respect		--	--	**	R	
	Social skills			--	--	**	R
	Team play					--	**
Locomotor	Run	**					
	Gallop	**					
	Hop	--	**				
	Slide	--	**				
	Skip		--	**			
	Leap			--	**		
	Long jump			--	**		
	Vertical jump			--	**		
Rhythm and dance	Even beat	**					
	Uneven beat	**					
	Accented beat	--	**				
	Communication through Movement	--	**				
	Polka			**			
	Schottische				**		
Body control	Log roll	**					
	Shoulder roll	--	**				
	Forward roll	--	**				
	Backward roll		--	**			
	Two-point balances		--	**			
	One-point balances			--	**		
	Rope jump		--	--	**		
	Balance beam walk		**				
	Cartwheel				--	**	
	Headstand				--	**	
Physical fitness	Partial curl-ups			**			
	Endurance run		--	--	--	--	**

16

Goal area	Objective	Grades					
		K	1	2	3	4	5
	Push-ups				--	--	**
	V-sit reach					--	**
	Body mass index						**
	Stretching	--	--	**	R	R	
	Warm-up	--	--	**	R	R	
	Active lifestyle					--	**
	Cardiorespiratory exertion	--	--	**	R	R	
Object control	Underhand roll	**					
	Underhand throw	**					
	Overhand throw		--	--	**		
	Catch	--	--	**			
	Fielding fly balls				--	**	
	Fielding ground balls			--	**		
	Two-arm sidearm strike		--	--	**		
	Forehand strike				--	**	
	Backhand strike					--	**
	Overhand strike					--	**
	Kick stationary ball	--	**				
	Kick moving ball	--	--	**			
	Trap ball		--	--	**		
	Throw-in				--	**	
	Foot dribble			--	--	**	
	Two-handed chest pass			--	--	**	
	Bounce pass			--	--	**	
	Hand dribble				R	--	**
	Set shot				--	--	**
	Forearm pass			--	--	**	
	Overhand pass				--	--	**
	Underhand strike			--	--	**	

** = Mastery expected by the end of this grade.

- - = Objective is introduced or worked on during this grade.

R = objective is reviewed or time is allocated for maintenance.

would be targeted for mastery at a much higher grade level. The goal of this step is to create a scope and sequence chart like the example shown in table 1.9. Remember that the majority of the objectives in the *Everyone Can* materials have three skill levels (see figure 1.1). The goal of the model program plan is for *all* students to master skill level 1 of all 66 objectives in the plan. The additional skill levels are provided for each objective to challenge the more skilled students and so a wide range of abilities can be addressed while working on the same objective.

Some teachers are surprised when they learn they have time to teach only a fraction of the number of objectives they attempted to teach in the past. Understand that if your calculations in step 3 indicated that you only have time to teach five objectives each year, you actually will be working on teaching many more objectives. Five is the number of objectives you are expected to have the students master each year. During each year of the program you will be introducing some new objectives, continuing work on others, and finishing instruction on the objectives targeted for mastery during that year. In table 1.9, dashes (–) indicate when instruction begins for each objective, and asterisks (**) indicate when the objective is targeted to be mastered. So in any given year, you will be working on all the objectives marked with either asterisks or dashes.

While teachers are usually given a fair amount of discretion when it comes to sequencing the content across the program based on their previous teaching experience, the ABC model does recommend three rules be used based on the previous steps in the planning process.

1. First, the program goal emphasis chart developed in step 2 should be used as a guide to ensure that the objectives are distributed across the program as initially intended.

2. Second, the average objective mastery times for the different types of objectives (see step 3) should be used as a guide for distributing the time allocated to each objective. If 600 minutes has been identified for teaching a specific objective such as catching, how should this time be distributed? Should 100 minutes be spent during each year, or would it be more appropriate to concentrate some of the time during certain grades?

For example, 250 minutes could be allocated to this objective in second and third grade and 50 minutes a year for fourth and fifth to focus on review and retention.

3. Third, a set number of objectives must be targeted to be mastered during each year of the program. At the end of step 3 you calculated the number of objectives that should be mastered during each year (or grade level) of the program. This is the number of objectives that should be targeted to be achieved by all students for each year in the program. Failure to systematically distribute the target mastery of the objectives can result in students making it to the end of the program only to learn that they have not mastered all the objectives and there is now no time left to address these deficits. For the model program plan presented in chapter 6, there are 66 objectives. This means all students are expected to achieve skill level 1 on the 11 objectives targeted for mastery during each year of the program

The initial K-5 program plan is the starting point for an ongoing dynamic process. The plan is considered functional because it is based on the actual amount of time available for instruction as well as the priorities (goals and percent emphasis) valued by the physical education staff that will implement the program. As the plan is implemented, it must be constantly evaluated based on student achievement and program evaluation data and revised to ensure it is achieving its stated goals.

STEP ⑥ CREATE YEARLY TEACHING LEARNING MAPS

The scope and sequence chart (see table 1.9) identifies what content needs to be addressed during each year of the program. The next step is to examine the content identified to be worked on during each year of the program. This includes the objectives targeted to be mastered as well as any objectives targeted to be introduced for continued instruction or for review. This process involves the identification and development of Yearly Teaching Learning Maps (YTLMs) for each year of the program. Each YTLM consists of compatible groupings of program objectives into theme blocks based on the amount of time allotted to teach each objective for that year. Typically, theme blocks range from two to eight weeks in length. Blocks can be the same length as the units that teachers normally teach.

The creation of the YTLMs largely depends on the competence and creativity of the teachers. Theme blocks can be developed and implemented by groups of teachers or independently by each teacher. Whether or not a theme block is effective—that is, whether students make meaningful gains—is the key criterion. Key considerations for creating theme blocks include the following:

1. Decide how often each objective needs to be worked on across the year. Remember the goal of using theme blocks rather then traditional units is to allow for objectives to be worked on more frequently. For example, it is common for many fitness objectives to be included in multiple themes across a given year.

2. Theme Block Sequencing and Scheduling
   a. Schedule outdoor blocks during the fall and spring when weather should interfere less with instruction.
   b. Schedule blocks according to seasonal activities (e.g., baseball in the spring).
   c. Schedule blocks according to availability of facilities (e.g., soccer when the athletic fields are available).
   d. Schedule blocks with objectives that are prerequisites to others earlier in the sequence (e.g., teaching hop before skip because skip involves a step-hop).

3. Instructional Compatibility of Objectives
   a. Performance objectives requiring similar equipment may be grouped together if appropriate (e.g., those requiring mats).
   b. Performance objectives can be grouped together based on whether they can be taught indoors or outdoors.
   c. Performance objectives may be grouped together by sport to compose an instructional block.
   d. Seasonal activities such as the overhand throw, horizontal jump, and run may be grouped as a track and field instructional block in the spring.

4. Time Allotments
   a. Use the estimates computed earlier for number of weeks and days per year for the instructional program or assign a length of time spent on a similar unit in the past, if possible.
   b. Some blocks will be longer or shorter than others because of the number of program objectives within the block or predetermined use of facilities.
   c. Some blocks will take less or more time to achieve gains because of difficulty of program objectives or performance level of the students in the class.

5. To avoid problems in learning, it might be preferable to avoid grouping skills that have similar components. For example, teaching the underhand and overhand throw at the same time can cause problems for low-skill students learning these skills.

Table 1.10 is an example of a YTLM for the fourth grade based on the model program example we have been using in this chapter. The table indicates that the first step toward creating a YTLM is to identify which objectives to address during the year for a given grade. The next step is to group the objectives and organize them into several logical themes. In the example in table 1.10, the year was divided into nine theme blocks of four weeks each. Again, any length blocks can be used, with shorter length theme blocks (four weeks or less) being preferred over longer blocks (six weeks or more) for many themes because they allow for the target objectives to be worked on in multiple blocks spread out over the year. Shorter blocks also provide greater variety, which enhances student motivation and interest. Note that the amount of time allotted to each objective in the program plan should be carefully considered during the planning process. Each objective should receive the appropriate amount of time for instruction and practice. This table is typically created using an Excel spreadsheet so teachers can later track how much time is spent on each objective. Of course once instruction begins some fluctuation in the amount of time spent on each objective will occur depending on the skill levels of the students.

After a YTLM is created for each year in the program, the next step is to create a Block Teaching Learning Map (BTLM) for each theme in the yearly maps. A sample BTLM is shown in table 1.11. The BTLM is simply further refinement of how instruction and time is allocated for each objective across the classes within a given theme block. Do not be concerned about dividing time into exact intervals and keeping track of how much time has been used for each objective. Time will be tracked via a spreadsheet in which defined functions can be set to do all the math (see Kelly and Melograno, 2004). Once you have created the BTLMs you have an outline for each of your lessons to use when you begin your implementation planning (discussed in chapter 3).

Table 1.10   Sample Yearly Teaching Learning Map for the Fourth Grade

Fourth-Grade Yearly Teaching Learning Map

Instructional Blocks—9 × 4 weeks

Objectives	Status	Ball Skills	Striking	X-Games	Ball Skills	Striking	X-Games	Ball Skills	Striking	Fitness
Social skills	M		X	O	O	O	O	O	O	O
Team play	I							X	O	O
Self-respect	R	X	O	O	O	O	O	O	O	O
Cartwheel	M			X			X			
Headstand	M			X			X			
Endurance run	I		X	O	O	O	O	O	O	O
Push-ups	I			X	O	O	O	O	O	O
V-sit	I			X	O	O	O	O	O	O
Active lifestyle	I		X							X
Stretching	R	X	O	O	O	O	O	O	O	O
Warm-up	R	X	O	O	O	O	O	O	O	O
CR exertion	R		X	O	O	O	O	O	O	X
Fielding fly balls	M	X			X			X		X
Foot dribble	M	X			X			X		X
Throw-in	M	X			X			X		X
Hand dribble	I	X			X			X		
Two-handed chest pass	M	X			X			X		X
Bounce pass	M	X			X			X		X
Set shot	I				X			X		

Objectives	Status	Ball Skills	Striking	X-Games	Ball Skills	Striking	X-Games	Ball Skills	Striking	Fitness
Forehand strike	M		X			X			X	X
Backhand strike	I		X			X			X	
Overhand strike	I		X			X			X	
Forearm Pass	M		X			X			X	X
Underhand strike	M		X			X			X	X
Overhead pass	I		X			X			X	

Status codes
M = to be mastered this year.
I = continued instruction during this year.
R = already mastered but reviewed this year.

Matrix codes
X = focus of instruction during this unit.
O = ongoing practice/review during this unit.

Table 1.11 Sample Block Teaching Learning Map

Instruction Block 1: Ball Skills

Objectives/ days	Week 1					Week 2					Week 3					Week 4				
	M	T	W	T	F	M	T	W	T	F	M	T	W	T	F	M	T	W	T	F
Self-respect	O	O	O	O	O	O	O	O	O	O	O	O	O	O	O	O	O	O	O	O
Stretching	O	O	O	O	O	O	O	O	O	O	O	O	O	O	O	O	O	O	O	O
Warm-up	O	O	O	O	O	O	O	O	O	O	O	O	O	O	O	O	O	O	O	O
Fielding fly balls																				
Foot dribble		A	F	P	P	F	P	P	P	P	F	P	P	R						
Throw-in				A	F	F	P	P	P	P	F	P	P	P	R					
Hand dribble														A	F	P	P	P	R	
Two-handed chest pass							A	F	P	P	P	F	P	P	P	P	R			
Bounce pass								A	F	P	P	F	P	P	P	P	P	R		

Matrix codes:
A = initial assessment.
F = formal instruction.
P = practice with ongoing assessment.
O = ongoing application with review as needed.
R = formal reassessment.

STEP ❼
IDENTIFY OBJECTIVE ASSESSMENT ITEMS AND CREATE SCORESHEETS

The last step in the program planning process is to define each objective in the program plan as a stand-alone objective assessment item. What does it mean if a teacher says a student has a good running pattern? Is a good running pattern for a first-grader the same as a good running pattern for a fifth-grader? What does a mature catching pattern mean? Does it mean students can catch a 10-inch (25-cm) playground ball thrown softly to them underhand from a distance of 10 feet (3 m) or does it mean they can move and catch a tennis ball thrown in a high lob to within 10 feet (3 m) of their starting position? What are students expected to demonstrate to show mastery of each objective? What are the essential components or focal points of each objective that must be learned to achieve mastery?

These are key questions to address when defining objectives so that the objectives function as criterion-referenced assessment items. Fortunately, all the objectives included in the model K-5 program have already been defined as criterion-referenced items in the *Everyone Can* online resource materials. Figure 1.1 on

page 7 shows an example *Everyone Can* objective assessment item (OAI) for the Catch objective. Note that the OAI is first divided into one or more skill levels, and then specific focal points are identified that define how the skill must be performed to achieve mastery of each skill level. It is critical to define an OAI for each objective in the program plan so that the objectives can be interpreted and evaluated the same by all teachers and students using the program. For the model program plan highlighted in this chapter and described in detail in chapter 6, *all* students are expected to master skill level 1 for all of the objectives. Skill levels 2 and 3 are provided to challenge the more skilled students while the other students are mastering the skill level 1 focal points. The assessment process is addressed in more detail in chapter 2. To complete the planning process, the last step is to develop a scoresheet for each OAI. The *Everyone Can* resource materials provide a detailed scoresheet for each objective. Figure 1.3 shows a scoresheet for the Catch OAI. Across the top of the form are prompts to remind the teacher of the essential focal points under each skill level. The form is also designed so that both entry and exit performance data can be collected for an entire class on one form. How to use the scoresheets for student assessment and evaluation is discussed in chapters 2 and 5.

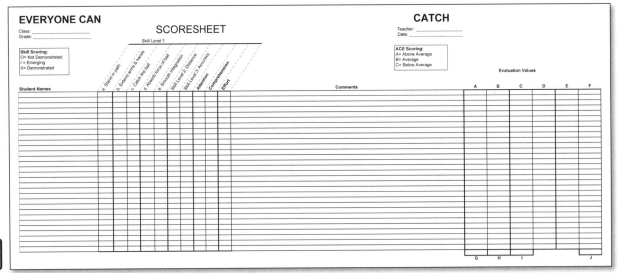

Figure 1.3 Detailed scoresheet for the Catch OAI.

SUMMARY

Many teachers are initially overwhelmed by the program planning process. Most assume that a program plan will be in place when they are hired and all they need to do is implement it. Ideally, this will be the case, but things sometimes fall short of ideal. In such a situation, you should now have a basic understanding of the steps you and your school need to take to develop a curriculum. Table 1.12 shows the relations among the chapter learning objectives and the program planning steps presented in this chapter. Review this table and reflect on your understanding.

The ABC model of instruction is designed to help you teach what and how you want so you can optimally address the physical education needs of your students. As such, the model is a procedural guide applicable to all levels of physical education (early childhood, elementary, secondary, and higher education) and any length of instructional unit (e.g., 1 hour, 1 day, 1 week, 1 term or semester). The model does not tell teachers what methods to employ, what instructional activities to use, or what specific learning tasks to assign students in the class. It simply presents a guide that teachers can use to systematically answer these questions:

- What should students learn?
- What instructional activities should be used?
- How do I determine whether students have learned what was taught?
- What changes need to be made?
- What options are available?

The ABC success cycle and program plan can also be used to assist teachers who have students with disabilities. The program plan scope and sequence and objective assessment items can be used to develop appropriate IEP long- and short-term instructional objectives. See chapter 7 for details on creating IEPs.

The high degree of structure of the ABC model of instruction can be disconcerting to some teachers initially. Our experience in curriculum development and program implementation has taught us that unless students master basic skills in a highly structured sequential context, there is little likelihood of them ever mastering more complex skills. We have found that most teachers who are initially concerned about this structured approach change their minds after they learn to implement the ABC model and their students start demonstrating improved skills.

Table 1.12   Program Planning Chapter Objectives and Planning Steps

Chapter learning objectives	Program planning steps	Chapter figures and tables
1. Know the steps involved in creating an ABC program plan.	1-7	
2. Explain the purpose of the program philosophy, program goals, and objectives in the ABC program planning process.	1	Tables 1.1, 1.2, 1.3
3. Understand the relations among program goal emphasis, average objective mastery time, and instruction time in program planning.	2,3,4	Tables 1.4, 1.5, 1.6, 2.7
4. Understand how to develop yearly program plans and sequential instruction blocks across time for the school year by grade.	5	Tables 1.3, 1.7, 1.8
5. Explain why program and block planning are fundamental for successful implementation of the ABC model of instruction.	6	Tables 1.8, 1.9, 1.10
6. Explain the importance of performance objectives in the implementation of the ABC model of instruction and how they are defined.	7	Figures 1.1, 1.2

In the ABC model of instruction, administrative and instructional accountability are built in and shared by teachers, students, administrators, parents, and the community. Allocation of facilities, resources, and equipment as well as teachers' time with students with disabilities can be determined most optimally when using the ABC program plan. Policies can be developed and implemented with an evaluation system incorporated to review and evaluate instruction, program effectiveness, administrative efficiency, facilities, and resources.

Home schooling is becoming more and more popular in many parts of the country, particularly at the elementary level. Many parents who are homeschooling their children contact their local school district for curricula guidance. The combination of your ABC program plan and the *Everyone Can* materials are excellent resources for these parents. Many home-schooled students will enter the regular education system at some later point in their education. If their parents have followed your ABC program plan, these students can transition smoothly into the school-based physical education curriculum.

We recommend that you complete this chapter's enrichment activities to self-evaluate your understanding of the material presented. Also, use the program plan self-monitoring form to review a local physical education curriculum and evaluate your understanding of the ABC planning components. The purpose of the enrichment activities and the self-monitoring form is to provide you with information to help you improve your planning. These are not tests, and no one expects perfection. Your goal is simply to continually improve the effectiveness and efficiency of your planning.

ENRICHMENT ACTIVITIES

These activities should help you understand the major concepts addressed in this chapter. Most teachers find it beneficial to actually interact with the content. These activities allow you to experiment with the content and see how it works in practice. The activities can be done individually or in small groups.

1. Contact a school system in your local area and ask if you can borrow a copy of their physical education curriculum. Use the program planning steps presented in this chapter to review this curriculum. Are the following pieces included?

   - Information on the curriculum committee?

   - Information on the program philosophy?

   - Information on the program goals? (Are there functional statements regarding what students will be able to do at the end of the program?)

   - A rank-ordered list of objectives to achieve each goal?

   - A program goal emphasis chart that indicates how much emphasis each goal will receive during each year of the program?

   - Amount of instruction time available for physical education?

   - Objective mastery time (estimated time needed to teach mastery of an average objective in the curriculum)?

   - A rationale for how much content is included in the curriculum?

   - A program scope and sequence chart that indicates when each objective in the curriculum will be mastered?

2. Take the program plan presented in chapter 6 and explain it to a school administrator, classroom teacher, or parent. What is their reaction? Can you answer their questions?

3. Contact a local elementary physical educator and ask the following questions about their physical education curriculum:

   - Who created it and when?

   - How closely do they follow the curriculum?

   - Approximately how many objectives do they attempt to teach each year?

- How much physical education (i.e., total time) does each grade received?

- What percentage of their students leave the program having mastered all the objectives in the curriculum? How do they know this?

- Do all elementary teachers in the district teach the same content?

Compare and discuss your results with peers. How many of the curricula reviewed meet the ABC program planning standards?

4. Using the program scope and sequence chart presented in table 1.9, pick a grade level and create your own yearly teaching learning map (YTLM). Compare your YTLM with your peers and discuss the similarities and differences.

5. Using either the YTLM presented in table 1.10 (p. 20) or the YTLM you created in enrichment activity 4, pick one of your theme blocks and develop a block teaching learning map (BTLM) for this block of instruction. Compare your BTLM with those of your peers and discuss the similarities and differences.

6. Three teachers are developing an elementary physical education curriculum for their school district. They identified four goal areas, and each teacher has decided how much emphasis each goal should receive in the program:

- Teacher 1: fitness (50%), object skills (25%), locomotor (15%), body awareness (10%)

- Teacher 2: object skills (50%), fitness (10%), locomotor (20%), body awareness (20%)

- Teacher 3: body awareness (25%), locomotor (25%), object skills (25%), fitness (25%)

Given this information, calculate the average goal emphasis for each goal in this program plan.

7. An elementary physical education program (grades 1-6) receives physical education three times a week for 20 minutes. How much instructional time is there in this program?

8. A teacher wants to calculate an average objective mastery time for a program she is developing. She has three goal areas in her program, with the following program goal emphases: object skills (50%), locomotor skills (27%), and fitness (23%). She picks a typical objective from each goal area and estimates how long she thinks it will take her to teach mastery of these objectives:

- Object skills—overhand throw: 620 minutes

- Locomotor skills—skip: 540 minutes

- Fitness—curl-ups: 360 minutes

Based on this information, what would the average objective mastery time be for her program?

9. A teacher has been developing a program plan for his K-5 elementary physical education program. He has defined five goals and created a rank-ordered list of objectives for each goal. He has calculated that he has a total of 12,000 minutes of instruction time allocated for his program and that his average objective mastery time is 600 minutes. If the average goal emphasis for object control skills in his program is 40 percent, how many objectives can he include in his program for this goal area?

10. Review the model K-5 program plan in chapter 6 and then answer these questions:

   a. How many objectives should students master in third grade? How is this number determined?

   b. What is the goal emphasis for rhythm and dance in this program plan?

   c. What is the average objective mastery estimate for object control skills?

   d. If the total amount of instruction time is increased for this program by 4,000 minutes, which of the following would have to be recalculated and why?

   - Goal emphasis

   - Average objective mastery

   - Number of objectives per goal area

Program Plans Monitor Form

Teacher's name: _____   Date: _____

INSTRUCTIONS

Use this form to evaluate how physical education curricula address the basic ABC program planning principles. Check the best response. (If your answer is other than Yes or No, explain your answer on a separate sheet of paper. Include the item number with your explanation.)

1. Is there a written program philosophy statement and set of physical education program goals that indicate what content will be achieved and that is based on the potential contributions of activity to the growth, development, and general quality of life for all students? ☐ Yes ☐ No

2. Are the goal statements written in output terminology (i.e., do they represent the results of instruction rather than instructional inputs or opportunities)? ☐ Yes ☐ No

3. Are the goals derived or created using both professional and community input to ensure their local relevance, and are they consistent with district, state, and national guidelines? ☐ Yes ☐ No

4. Is there a written document that identifies program objectives that operationally define each goal statement? ☐ Yes ☐ No

5. Is the relative importance of each program goal reflected in the number of objectives that are included in the program plan? ☐ Yes ☐ No

6. Are the total number of objectives included in the program based on time available and time needed for students to achieve mastery? ☐ Yes ☐ No

7. Is there a scope and sequence chart that indicates when instruction will begin and when mastery is expected for each objective in the program? ☐ Yes ☐ No

   a. Is the number of objectives included based on a match between instruction time available and time needed for students to achieve mastery? ☐ Yes ☐ No

   b. Do the yearly program plans build on the previous year and provide the foundation for the next year in the program? ☐ Yes ☐ No

8. Are all objectives operationally defined and have a sufficient range in difficulty to provide for the assessment of students who range in performance ability from near zero competence to functional competence or mastery? ☐ Yes ☐ No

9. Are the program objectives organized into a written curriculum structure that identifies a logical progression of program objectives for each grade in the program as well as when instruction begins on each objective and when each objective is to be mastered? ☐ Yes ☐ No

10. Is there a yearly teaching learning map for each year in the program plan? ☐ Yes ☐ No

    a. Are all performance objectives in the yearly program plan listed? ☐ Yes ☐ No

    b. Are performance objectives logically grouped into instructional blocks? ☐ Yes ☐ No

    c. Are instructional blocks logically sequenced across the school year? ☐ Yes ☐ No

ASSESSMENT

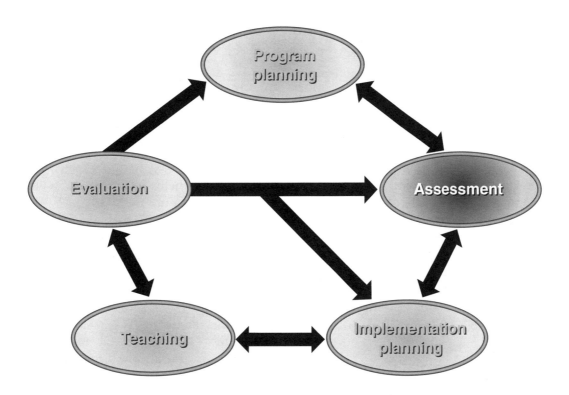

Once you have developed an ABC program plan, you know when each objective should be taught. The next step in preparing for the teaching process is assessment. For some, assessment can have a negative connotation. Some teachers view assessment as a time-consuming process that wastes their valuable instruction time, and many students associate assessment with being tested and graded. In this chapter we hope you will learn to view assessment differently.

During assessment using the ABC model teachers discover which skills each student already knows or can perform correctly for the objectives targeted for instruction as well as which focal points of the objectives each student still needs to work on. For teachers, assessment is the key for planning and implementing daily instruction so that all students achieve the objectives targeted in the curriculum. For students, assessment is the key to knowing what they need to practice and how to correct errors in performance.

After reading this chapter, you should be able to . . .

1. Explain the role and importance of assessment in the ABC success cycle.

2. Explain how the *Everyone Can* objective assessment items are defined as criterion-referenced assessment instruments.

3. Demonstrate how to score and record student assessment data on a scoresheet.

4. Explain the process for selecting an appropriate assessing activity.

5. Demonstrate how to implement an assessment activity.

6. Explain different strategies for assessing and recording student performance.

Assessment in the ABC model has two distinct differences from the traditional summative once- or twice-a-year assessment methods commonly used in physical education. First, assessment in the ABC model is curriculum embedded. This means you assess directly what you teach. Second, assessment in the ABC model is an ongoing process that occurs every day. Assessment is not a separate process performed occasionally when time permits but an integral part of the learning process that precedes and follows all instruction. The ABC assessment process involves six steps.

Assessment Steps

1. Determine what objectives should be assessed.
2. Select an appropriate assessment instrument.
3. Score and record performance.
4. Select an assessment activity.
5. Conduct an assessment activity.
6. Conduct other forms of assessment.

STEP ❶
DETERMINE WHAT OBJECTIVES SHOULD BE ASSESSED

Determining which objectives to assess can easily be done by viewing the ABC plan outlined in chapter 1 and presented in detail in chapter 6 (see the model K-5 physical education program plan). After objectives are identified and sequenced across the grades in the program, they are grouped into theme blocks for each grade. Table 1.9 (p. 15) shows a sample yearly teaching learning map (YTLM) for fourth-grade students. As you may recall, the YTLMs are further broken down into block teaching learning maps (BTLMs). To determine which objectives to assess, teachers simply review the BTLM and identify which objectives are targeted for instruction in the next block. Examining the BTLM shown in table 2.1, we see the teacher needs to assess the foot dribble and throw-in during the first week of the first instruction block.

STEP ❷
SELECT AN APPROPRIATE ASSESSMENT INSTRUMENT

What defines a good throw or a mature skipping pattern? How are "good" and "mature" defined so that all teachers working on the same objectives are teaching the same thing? In the ABC model these questions are answered by defining each program objective in the curriculum as a *criterion-referenced assessment instrument*. Each program objective is defined in terms of one or more skill levels. The first skill level defines the mature pattern in terms of critical performance criteria, called focal points. Each focal point represents an observable element of the objective

Table 2.1 Sample Block Teaching Learning Map

Instruction Block 1: Ball Skills

Objectives/ days	Week 1					Week 2					Week 3					Week 4				
	M	T	W	T	F	M	T	W	T	F	M	T	W	T	F	M	T	W	T	F
Self-respect	O	O	O	O	O	O	O	O	O	O	O	O	O	O	O	O	O	O	O	O
Stretching	O	O	O	O	O	O	O	O	O	O	O	O	O	O	O	O	O	O	O	O
Warm-up	O	O	O	O	O	O	O	O	O	O	O	O	O	O	O	O	O	O	O	O
Fielding fly balls																				
Foot dribble		A	F	P	P	F	P	P	P	P	F	P	P	R						
Throw-in				A	F	F	P	P	P	P	F	P	P	P	R					
Hand dribble														A	F	P	P	P	R	
Two-handed chest pass						A	F	P	P	P	F	P	P	P	P	P	R			
Bounce pass							A	F	P	P	F	P	P	P	P	P	P	R		

Matrix codes:

A = initial assessment.

F = formal instruction.

P = practice with ongoing assessment.

O = ongoing application with review as needed.

R = formal reassessment.

that is essential for performing the overall skill. This is the skill level that *all* students are expected to master in the program. Many performance objectives have additional skill levels that assess the application of the skill.

Figure 2.1 shows the objective assessment item (OAI) for the overhand throw. The first section (top of the form) tells you the name of the objective and the equipment and space required to administer this OAI. The second section defines the skill levels down the left side of the form. The first skill level of all the assessment items, skill level 1, focuses on how the basic skill is performed. The second and third skill levels concern applications of skill level 1. For example, skill level 1 of the overhand throw focuses on mechanically throwing correctly, whereas skill levels 2 and 3 focus on the use of the skill level 1 pattern to throw for distance and accuracy.

The third section of the assessment item defines the OAI's focal points, which are the critical performance criteria a student must demonstrate to perform the skill correctly. The skill level 1 focal points define specific performance

criteria regarding how the skill is performed (e.g., feet apart, weight transfer, follow through). For the overhand throw example shown in figure 2.1, students must demonstrate seven focal points on two out of three trials to earn mastery of skill level 1. The skill level 2 and 3 focal points can be either more advanced performance criteria or, more commonly, product measures for distance and accuracy, as illustrated in the overhand throw example.

The *Everyone Can* assessment items are designed to be both representative of the content covered in elementary physical education and comprehensive of the range of abilities commonly found in typical classes. The goal of the physical education program is to teach all students the skill level 1 competencies—that is, how to perform the basic skills. However, in a typical physical education class it is not uncommon to learn after your initial assessment that while the majority of the class needs work on several of the skill level 1 focal points, a few other students have already mastered these points. Here is where the skill level 2 and 3 criteria come into play. Use the criteria defined

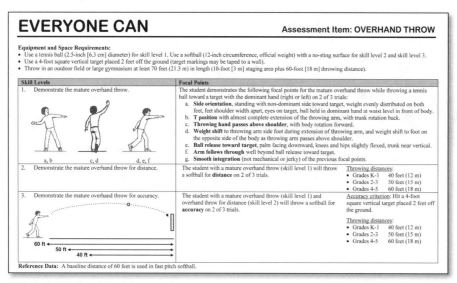

EVERYONE CAN   Assessment Item: OVERHAND THROW

Equipment and Space Requirements:
- Use a tennis ball (2.5-inch [6.3 cm] diameter) for skill level 1. Use a softball (12-inch circumference, official weight) with a no-sting surface for skill level 2 and skill level 3.
- Use a 4-foot square vertical target placed 2 feet off the ground (target markings may be taped to a wall).
- Throw in an outdoor field or large gymnasium at least 70 feet (21.3 m) in length (10-foot [3 m] staging area plus 60-foot [18 m] throwing distance).

Skill Levels	Focal Points

1. Demonstrate the mature overhand throw.	The student demonstrates the following focal points for the mature overhand throw while throwing a tennis ball toward a target with the dominant hand (right or left) on 2 of 3 trials:
	  a. **Side orientation**, standing with non-dominant side toward target, weight evenly distributed on both feet, feet shoulder width apart, eyes on target, ball held in dominant hand at waist level in front of body.
	  b. **T position** with almost complete extension of the throwing arm, with trunk rotation back.
	  c. **Throwing hand passes above shoulder**, with body rotation forward.
	  d. **Weight shift** to throwing arm side foot during extension of throwing arm, and weight shift to foot on the opposite side of the body as throwing arm passes above shoulder.
	  e. **Ball release toward target**, palm facing downward, knees and hips slightly flexed, trunk near vertical.
	  f. **Arm follows through** well beyond ball release toward target.
	  g. **Smooth integration** (not mechanical or jerky) of the previous focal points.

2. Demonstrate the mature overhand throw for distance.	The student with a mature overhand throw (skill level 1) will throw a softball for **distance** on 2 of 3 trials. Throwing distances:
	  • Grades K-1 40 feet (12 m)
	  • Grades 2-3 50 feet (15 m)
	  • Grades 4-5 60 feet (18 m)

3. Demonstrate the mature overhand throw for accuracy.	The student with a mature overhand throw (skill level 1) and overhand throw for distance (skill level 2) will throw a softball for **accuracy** on 2 of 3 trials. Accuracy criterion: Hit a 4-foot square vertical target placed 2 feet off the ground.
	
	Throwing distances:
	  • Grades K-1 40 feet (12 m)
	  • Grades 2-3 50 feet (15 m)
	  • Grades 4-5 60 feet (18 m)

Reference Data: A baseline distance of 60 feet is used in fast pitch softball.

Figure 2.1 Overhand throw assessment.

Illustrations reprinted from J. Wessel, 1976, *I can: Object control* (North Brook, IL: Hubbard Scientific Company), 35. By permission of J. Wessel.

in levels 2 and 3 to challenge the high-skilled students and monitor their progress while the other students are learning the skill level 1 focal points. Yes, it would be ideal for all students to leave the program demonstrating all skill levels for all objectives, but given the limited time available for instruction in physical education, that is not realistic in many programs. In these cases, the goal should be that all students master at least the skill level 1 performance level for all objectives in the physical education curriculum.

The OAIs for the 70 objectives included in the model ABC program plan are presented in the online resources. These items were developed and then validated by comparisons with the existing motor development literature by panels of experts—and more important by practicing teachers. The items are authentic and curriculum embedded; they are direct measures of what students do in physical education, sports, and games. The number of focal points or criteria used to define a skill can be expanded or contracted depending on the purpose of the assessment item. Many assessments, designed to serve primarily as evaluative measures to determine whether students have met established benchmarks such as NASPE's (2008) PE-Metircs, use only a small number of criteria to define each objective. The *Everyone Can* OAIs tend to be more detailed and contain a greater number of focal points because they are designed to guide instruction. These

OAIs can also be adapted or modified using task analysis procedures for expansion or contraction of the skill levels or focal points to meet the specific needs of a given student. Many students with disabilities, for example, will learn at a slower rate and might require that the focal points be further delineated into smaller components. For example, using the throw definition in figure 2.1, the first focal point could be divided into two subpoints: side orientation and eyes on target. The smaller components make it easier to focus instruction, show progress, and motivate students who learn at a slower rate.

The focal points are discrete components of the OAIs. They serve as criterion measures by which performance is assessed in *Everyone Can*. The focal points within a skill level are not necessarily sequential. The focal points for most of the skills are listed in the sequence in which they occur when they are performed correctly. This is not necessarily the same order in which the focal points are developmentally acquired or should be taught. For example, when catching, a student might demonstrate correct arm extension (focal point b) and ball contact (focal point d) without demonstrating the correct preparatory position (focal point a).

It is easy to grasp the concept of criterion-referenced assessment with the *Everyone Can* OAIs, but it takes some practice to be able to quickly and accurately assess a class of students using these instruments. One of the keys to being able to assess efficiently is knowing the focal points of the OAI you are using. This does not mean reading them a couple times before you start assessing. The first time you are using a new OAI for a given objective you must memorize the focal points and then practice observing them. If you find you have to repeatedly refer to the focal point descriptions to remember what to observe, you are not ready to assess. The goal is to watch the whole performance and then judge which components were performed consistently (i.e., two out of three times). Contrast this with watching the student several times while checking a single focal point for each observation—a far less efficient method of assessment.

By studying the skill level focal points and practicing assessing, teachers should be able to observe and reliably evaluate the students in their classes. One recommended procedure is to practice assessing with a colleague by observing students (live or on video) and then comparing and discussing the results. Other ways to practice assessing are to view sports on television, observe children at play, or have colleagues perform the skills with various errors to see if you can detect them. Research (Kelly and Moran, In Press; Walkley and Kelly, 1990) has shown that reasonable levels of accuracy and reliability can be obtained by teachers using criterion-referenced items like the *Everyone Can* OAIs after three to four hours of practice per objective (with feedback and once focal points have been memorized).

It is extremely important in the ABC model to change students' views of both assessment and instruction. Students should not view assessment as being tested or graded but as a learning tool. Students should understand that to learn a new skill they need to know what focal points they need work on as well as feedback on how they are doing while practicing these focal points. The role of the teacher changes from disciplinarian and grader to the expert who provides continuous feedback that enables students to improve performance.

STEP ❸
SCORE AND RECORD PERFORMANCE

Probably the greatest challenge to getting teachers to integrate assessment into their instruction is getting them to regularly record their assessment data. This is a legitimate concern when you consider many elementary physical education teachers may teach 300 to 500 students a week. Ideally, teachers will assess and record student performance daily. When this is not practical, teachers must record assessment data at least at the beginning and end of each instructional block. The downside of recording data only at the beginning and end of a block is that if you find that students did not improve at the end of the block, you have used up all your instruction time. Teachers are thus encouraged to record assessment data as often as possible. To ease this process, we provide a scoresheet for each *Everyone Can* OAI. Simply duplicate the sheets you need to accommodate the number of students in your class. A detailed scoresheet for the overhand throw is shown in figure 2.2.

The columns of figure 2.2 are designed to collect four types of data. The first several columns contain students' names and a place to record whether students have demonstrated each skill level and focal point. The column header for each of the focal point columns contains a brief (two to four words) phrase to identify the focal point. Note that the words composing the focal point labels are in bold in the assessment item definitions. These labels are only prompts; you need to know all of the performance criteria defined for each focal point in the objective assessment item definition. For example, focal point e for skill level 1 of the overhand throw states, "Ball release toward target, palm facing downward, knees and hips slightly flexed, trunk near vertical." The label for this focal point on the scoresheet is "Ball released toward target."

Following the skill performance columns are three columns in which to record student attention, comprehension, and effort (called ACE behaviors) during the assessment. A scoring rubric for rating these behaviors is at the top of the form. The ACE ratings provide simple indicators of whether the behavior observed is an accurate picture of student ability. If students receive A ratings for the ACE behaviors, it can be assumed that the assessed performance is probably a good indicator of current ability. However, if students are perceived to have been confused or distracted or to have given a half-hearted effort during assessment, their ACE ratings would remind the teacher to interpret their assessment performance cautiously.

In the third section of the scoresheet the teacher enters comments. This space is used to record information unique to each student that might be related to a specific error they are

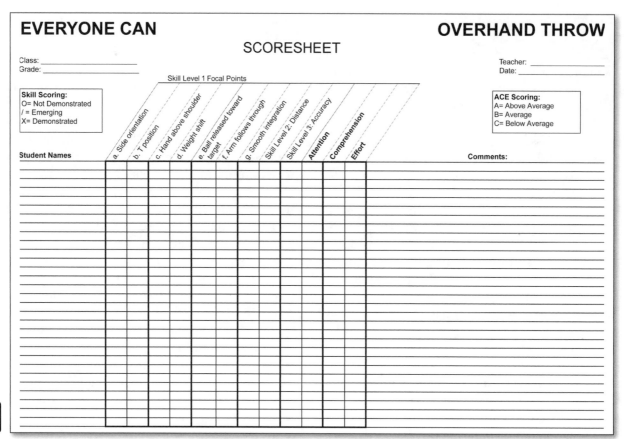

Figure 2.2   Overhand throw scoresheet.

making or to remind the teacher of an instructional need to consider during implementation planning. Finally, the last set of columns is used for student evaluation. These will be addressed in chapter 5 on evaluation.

In addition to knowing the focal points of the objective being assessed, you must also know how to efficiently record information on the scoresheets. The first task is getting all student names on the forms. They should be grouped and listed in a manner that allows for quick access (e.g., by squads or alphabetically). Electronic versions of the scoresheets are provided on the online resource. Teachers who have access to electronic copies of their class lists can cut and paste them into the scoresheets and print them for use in their classes.

X / O Method

A scoring rubric is provided at the top right of the scoresheet for scoring and recording student performance on the focal points. If a focal point

is not demonstrated, it is scored an O. If a focal point is partially demonstrated but could be improved with additional instruction, it is scored a slash (/). Finally, if the focal point is demonstrated correctly on two of three trials it is scored an X. The advantage of this scoring system is that the same scoresheet can be used for multiple reassessments of the same class. When a previously undemonstrated focal point begins to be partially demonstrated, the teacher can mark a / over the O. Later, when the student can consistently perform the focal point, the teacher can convert the / into an X.

Alternative Scoring Procedures

Teachers are encouraged to adopt a scoring and recording process that works for them. In addition to the X/O method just described, other common methods that can be used on the *Everyone Can* scoresheets are described here.

Date Method

When a focal point is mastered the date is entered (month/year: 02/21); otherwise leave the cell blank. Dates are filled in the appropriate focal point boxes as students achieve the various focal points not demonstrated during the initial assessment of the instructional block. An advantage of this method is that it provides information on how much time passes before the focal point was achieved.

X Only Method

Here nothing is recorded in the box for a focal point until the student demonstrates mastery. This method is quick and promotes a tidy, easy-to-read scoresheet. The downside is it collects only the minimal amount of information, which limits interpreting progress and how much change occurs over time.

Skill Rubrics

This method is similar to the X/O method, but numbers or letters are entered as codes to indicate information about the consistency or quality of the movement. Here are two common examples:

0 = no evidence	a = not demonstrated
1 = occasionally	b = attempts to perform
2 = usually	c = rudimentary performance
3 = always	mance
	d = correct performance

Multiple Baseline

For many students with disabilities, performance can vary tremendously from day to day. In such cases, it is valuable to collect performance data across several days and then view this information collectively when assessing present level of performance on an objective. A separate scoresheet is used for each student. Instead of listing names in the first column, list the dates you reassessed the student on. After each assessment period, draw a dark line to indicate where the next assessment block begins.

Retention

Some students have problems retaining skills they have learned over time. The retention scor-

ing method is the same as the multiple baseline method described previously, but here the student is reassessed over the course of one or more weeks (or months or years) to monitor retention. A separate scoresheet is used for each student. Instead of listing names in the first column, list the dates you reassessed the student. After each assessment period, draw a dark line to indicate where the next assessment block begins.

Recommendations for Assessment

The ABC model recommends establishing a systematic procedure to ensure all students are periodically reassessed. Our research shows that unless teachers systematically observe their students, they are not truly aware of how well or poorly the students are doing on the objectives they are teaching. This is because the better-performing students tend to demand and subsequently receive more of the teacher's attention, whereas the poor-performing students tend to avoid being observed by the teacher. These students frequently stop to tie their shoes or choose to chase down their balls when it is their turn to be observed. Unless the teacher has a plan to ensure that all students are regularly observed, they might very well be manipulated by their students. When time is limited or when teachers have large classes, a common method to monitor student performance is to pick three or four students randomly from the class list before each class. The teacher then observes (assesses) these students during the drills and activities and uses their performance and progress as a predictor of how the class is progressing overall on the objectives being taught.

STEP ❹ SELECT AN ASSESSMENT ACTIVITY

One of the major concerns teachers have about teaching with the ABC model is that the approach focuses so much on assessing, which is very time consuming. Assessing students does require time, which might be wasted time if the assessment data are not directly related to what is being taught and are not used to plan and implement instruction.

ABC assessment is an integral part of teaching and not a separate procedure done a few times a year to record scores on paper. To effectively teach students a skill, the teacher must first observe (assess) students to determine where they are on the objective being taught—what focal points do they already know, and which do they need to work on? This assessment is used to plan the initial instruction for the objective. Then, during instruction, the teacher continually assesses the students to provide them with feedback on what is being done right and wrong.

Another way to look at the assessment process and the issue of time is to consider what teachers are going to do with the time they save by neglecting to assess. Although not assessing students might initially save some time, without assessment data the teacher has no means of planning appropriate instruction to meet the students' needs or for giving feedback during instruction. The time saved by not assessing thus results in wasting much subsequent instruction time because the teacher does not know precisely what students need to learn.

As discussed in step 3, it is necessary to formally assess all students in a class and record at least their entry and exit performance for each objective. The entry assessment establishes a baseline, and the exit assessment indicates progress made during the instruction block. During instruction, teachers need to continually assess to provide students with feedback and to evaluate the effectiveness of their daily instruction. Because the entry and exit measures are compared to determine student progress and the overall effectiveness of the instruction block, we recommend that these assessments be conducted under similar circumstances so any changes can be attributed to changes in student performance rather than in assessment procedure. To this end, a sample assessing activity is provided for each *Everyone Can* OAI.

Figure 2.3 illustrates the assessing activity provided for the overhand throw.

The first part of the form reviews the general instructions for conducting an assessment of the target objective. These instructions include administration reminders such as where to stand and what to say to students. They also remind the teacher to record the students' ACE behaviors (attention, comprehension, effort). Finally, they remind teachers that when there is any doubt that a student is successfully performing a focal point, they should not give credit. This is an important rule to remember. If students are not given credit for a focal point, they will be targeted to receive instruction on this focal point. If in fact they can already perform the focal point in question, the worst that can happen is that they will succeed on the activities planned for instruction until the teacher reassesses them and moves them to another focal point. On the other hand, if they are given credit for a focal point they have not truly mastered, they will not receive instruction on this focal point and will be expected to work on the next focal point, which they are not ready to learn. In this case, they might very well fail at the planned activities until the teacher reassesses them and corrects the situation. When in doubt, always err on the side of the students succeeding over failing.

The second part of the assessment activity provides instructions for how to involve students in a way that allows the teacher to assess performance. The goal of all assessments is to involve students

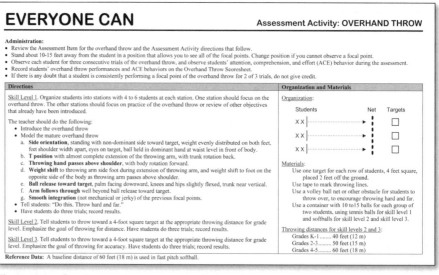

Figure 2.3 Overhand throw assessment activity.

in an activity that is both fun and engaging and also frees the teacher up to observe students on the objective being assessed. To the degree possible, assessing activities should elicit the students' natural performance or the way they normally perform the skill in everyday activities. You want to avoid contrived or pressure situations in which students try to perform the way they think you want them to perform, which might not indicate their actual ability.

The *Everyone Can* assessment activities are examples to provide teachers with a starting point. You are encouraged to modify the activities or to create your own. When creating your own assessment activity, follow these guidelines:

1. Make sure students understand the skill they should be performing while doing the activity.

2. An appropriate assessment activity frees the teacher up to move around and efficiently assess all students' performance for the selected objective.

3. The assessment activity should maximize student involvement and minimize the number of students waiting and watching. An audience can have a negative effect on student performance. Students waiting to be assessed without any structured activity tend to become restless and might disrupt the rest of the class.

4. Consider and control for other factors that might inhibit student performance such as fear, inappropriate dress, or social pressure.

5. Choose as natural a setting as possible to assess in. Try having students play a large class game or activity that involves many repetitions of the target objective.

STEP ❺
CONDUCT AN ASSESSMENT ACTIVITY

Once you have selected an assessment activity, review the instructions and organize your materials to prepare to conduct your assessment. The instructions on the assessment activities include a list of materials and hints on organizing the class.

Here are the administration instructions for the overhand throw:

- Select an overhand throwing activity or series of stations, one of which involves throwing a ball hard and far.
- Stand on the student's dominant side and slightly in front of the student at a distance that allows you to see all of the focal points.
- Instruct the students to throw the ball as far and as hard as they can on each throw.
- Have the students use a ball the size of a tennis ball.
- Observe each student for three consecutive trials of the overhand throw.
- Observe students' ACE behavior during the assessment.
- Record students' overhand throw performances and ACE behaviors on the scoresheet.
- If there is any doubt about a student consistently performing a focal point of the overhand throw, do not give credit.

Assessing is different from teaching. Be careful not to teach while conducting initial and final assessments. During assessments, you are interested in knowing what the students can do, not what they can learn while being assessed. Demonstrate the skill for the student by first saying, "Watch me do this." Observe the student's response and score. When possible, observe several repetitions (three or more performances) before scoring results. When using large-group activities for assessment, model the skill for students before starting the activity.

Students need to know what you are doing when you are assessing and why. You cannot stand on the sidelines looking at the students and writing things on a clipboard and expect students to act and perform naturally. Students almost always know when they are being observed, but they frequently do not know why or what is being observed. When using the ABC model this is not a secret. Students should understand at the start of an instruction block what objectives they will be working on and, based on the initial assessment, where they are on each objective and what they need to learn next. Throughout the block they have received feedback on the focal points they need to work on. Now at the end of the block you are recording where they are so you know where to continue their instruction when you return to this objective in a later block.

STEP ⑥
CONDUCT OTHER FORMS OF ASSESSMENT

Occasionally physical educators must evaluate a new student or, more commonly, evaluate a student with a disability to determine the most appropriate physical education placement. For example, let's say that a student with Down syndrome, Mary, has registered to attend your school and the principal asks you to determine whether to include her in Ms. Smith's second-grade class or Ms. Garcia's third-grade class. How would you make this decision?

Using the ABC model, you would conduct a general needs assessment. To do this, all you need is your ABC scope and sequence plan (table 1.10, p. 20) and your OAIs (see online resources). You need to determine whether Mary is ready to learn the physical education content targeted for second or third grade, so you first review the program plan and identify the objectives students are expected to master for each of these grades. The objectives are shown below by goal and grade level.

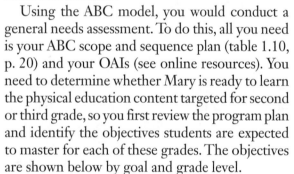

Second Grade	*Third Grade*
Personal space	Self-respect
Skip	Leap
Polka	Long jump
Backward roll	Vertical jump
Two-point balances	Schottische
Partial curl-ups	One-point balances
Stretching	Rope jump
Warm-up	Overhand throw
Cardiorespiratory exertion	Fielding ground balls
Catch	Two-hand sidearm strike
Kick moving ball	Foot trap

Depending on the number of objectives in your program plan and the amount of time available

for conducting your needs assessment, you can include all the target objectives in your assessment or pick one from each goal area for each grade. In our example, if time allows, you might start your assessment with the second-grade objectives. If Mary does poorly on these, it is very unlikely she would be successful on the third-grade objectives. Of course if she performs poorly on the second-grade objectives, you would need to go back and assess her on the first-grade objectives.

A general needs assessment is typically done in a relaxed one-on-one setting. After spending a few minutes to get to know Mary, you would ask her if she would play a game with you and show you some of her physical education skills. In a simple game of Show and Go, you can demonstrate a skill and ask Mary if she can do what you just did. Start with the easiest objectives and, if she has success, ask her to progress to the higher developmental objectives. The goal is to make this a positive experience for Mary. For this to happen, you must control the amount of success and failure she experiences. If Mary can demonstrate all the components of the hop, you will then ask her to skip. Conversely, if she cannot hop, there is no need to ask her to skip. To keep Mary motivated you might alternate who leads in the Show and Go so she has a chance to show you what she can do.

SUMMARY

Assessment is a decision-making process that allows teachers to determine where students are and what they need to learn on the objectives targeted for instruction in the ABC program plans. In the ABC model, assessment instruments are criteria referenced and embedded in the curriculum via the OAI definitions. The objectives are defined in terms of skill levels and focal points. The first skill level of each OAI defines the pattern, and subsequent skill levels define applications of this pattern, such as accuracy and distance. Within skill levels are focal points that indicate the distinct components of the skill being assessed. An OAI is provided for all 66 objectives in the model K-5 program plan in chapter 6; four additional fitness objectives are included in the online resource.

In the ABC model, assessment is an integral part of the teaching–learning process, not a procedure done only once or twice a year. Teachers assess on a daily basis to guide their instructional planning and provide students with meaningful feedback. An *Everyone Can* scoresheet is provided for each OAI and is designed to collect information on student skill level, focal point performance, and ACE behaviors and to allow for individual comments on students. Although we strongly recommend that student assessment data be collected and recorded on a daily basis, the bare minimum to record is the entry and exit performance measures for each objective during an instruction block. Assessment data are collected during an assessing activity designed to evaluate student performance in as natural a setting as possible. To be successful at assessing, teachers must learn the focal points of each objective and practice observing them before conducting their initial assessment. Finally, the *Everyone Can* OAIs and the ABC program plan can be used in concert to create a general needs assessment tool. You can use the general needs assessment to determine the appropriateness of a target placement for an individual student or the readiness of a student or group of students to learn a set of objectives targeted for instruction in the curriculum.

Complete the enrichment activities to self-evaluate your understanding of the material presented in this chapter. These activities provide you with feedback so that you can improve your assessing. Also ask a colleague to evaluate you using the assessment self-monitoring form at the end of the chapter.

ENRICHMENT ACTIVITIES

These activities should help you understand the major concepts addressed in this chapter. Most teachers find it beneficial to actually interact with the content. The activities allow you to experiment with the content and see how it works in practice. Do the activities individually or in small groups.

1. Interview a few teachers regarding how they value and use assessment in physical education. Ask them:
   - When and why do they assess?
   - How much time do they spend on assessing?
   - How do they record their assessment results?
   - What do they do with their assessment data?

2. Observe a teacher assessing students in physical education; then answer these questions:
   - What objectives or behaviors were being assessed?
   - Were the objectives or behaviors clearly defined?
   - Did the assessment focus on the process (how the skill was performed) or the product (the outcome of the skill performance)?
   - Was information recorded on the students' ACE behaviors?
   - Was the assessment done in a natural setting?
   - Overall, how did students respond?

3. Select an *Everyone Can* objective, but do not look at it. Break the skill down into its component parts and then compare your task analysis of the skill with the focal points provided in the *Everyone Can* materials. Share and discuss your task analysis and compare it with others created by students in your class.

4. With a partner, informally observe elementary school students playing or practicing motor skills (e.g., an after-school youth soccer practice). Select an appropriate *Everyone Can* assessment item and then both of you observe and assess the same student. Compare and discuss your results. Did you know the focal points well enough

or did you have to repeatedly reread them and then observe the student again? Based on this experience, how much practice do you think you need before you are ready to efficiently assess an entire class?

5. In interviews with elementary school students, ask them their views on the purpose of assessment and what they try to do when being assessed.

6. Plan and implement an assessment lesson and then evaluate your performance using the assessment-monitoring form.

7. A new student with a disability has entered your school. Your principal has asked you to evaluate this student to determine the most appropriate physical education placement. Explain how you design and implement this assessment.

Assessment Monitor Form

Teacher's name: _____   Date: _____

Check the appropriate response.

1. Have you identified the objectives that need to be assessed for the upcoming instructional block? ☐ Yes ☐ No

2. Do you know the skill levels and focal points to be assessed? Make sure you understand the skill levels and focal points and can observe them without repeatedly looking at the scoresheet for the focal point prompts. ☐ Yes ☐ No

3. Have you entered and organized the student names on the scoresheet to maximize efficiency during assessment? ☐ Yes ☐ No

4. Have you studied the scoresheet to make sure you understand the cue words on the scoresheet that relate to the focal points? ☐ Yes ☐ No

5. Did you have some form of written assessment activity? ☐ Yes ☐ No

6. Did you record each student's performance and ACE scores on the scoresheet during assessment? ☐ Yes ☐ No

7. Have you completed a scoresheet for every performance objective taught thus far? ☐ Yes ☐ No

8. Did you use correct (or equivalent) recording symbols? ☐ Yes ☐ No

9. Did all your recorded assessments meet the stated performance objective standards? ☐ Yes ☐ No

10. Did you modify focal points that were inappropriate for individual students (e.g., a student using a wheelchair)? ☐ Yes ☐ No

11. Did you start each assessing activity by providing a demonstration of the skill for your students? ☐ Yes ☐ No

12. Did your assessing activities allow you to maintain a clear view of the students being assessed? ☐ Yes ☐ No

13. Did you keep all students practicing the performance objective at least 50 percent of the class time during the assessment lesson? ☐ Yes ☐ No

14. When engaged in assessing, did you make full use of aides, assistants, or peer tutors available? ☐ Yes ☐ No

CHAPTER 3

IMPLEMENTATION PLANNING

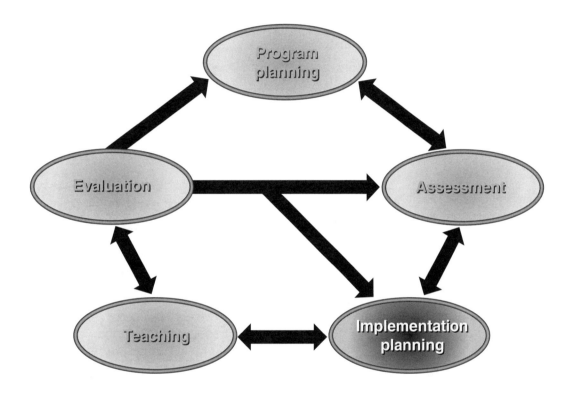

In **chapter 1** we used the ABC planning process to define our physical education curriculum. This process produced a number of products designed to guide the implementation of the program. First, it produced a scope and sequence chart (see table 1.9, p. 15) that indicated what content was included in the curriculum, when it would be taught, and when students were expected to master the content. Second, it illustrated how to identify all the objectives targeted to be addressed in a given year of the program and develop a yearly teaching learning map (YTLM) (table 1.10,

p. 20). The content identified in the YTLM was organized around instructional themes into small units called blocks. A block teaching learning map (BTLM) was then created for each theme in the YTLM (table 1.11, p. 21). Then in chapter 2 we learned that the first lesson of every BTLM is an assessment lesson in which students are observed on the objective assessment items for that block and their present level of performance recorded on a scoresheet. The focus of this chapter is to learn how to use this initial assessment data to plan your daily instruction.

CHAPTER OBJECTIVES

After reading this chapter you should be able to . . .

1. Explain the relation between YTLMs and BTLMs in the implementation planning process.

2. Demonstrate how to set initial learning expectations and target learning expectations and how to use these in evaluation.

3. Identify unique student learning needs and how to address them in the implementation planning process.

4. Create student instructional groupings for teaching based on student assessment data.

5. Explain the scope and content of the *Everyone Can* resource materials and how to use them to address the assessed needs of your students.

6. Create a teaching template and a student learning format based on the assessed needs of a class of students.

Planning instruction is like planning a trip using a map. You have to know where you want to go, where you are starting from, and the path you are going to take to reach your destination. The ABC planning process identifies what content needs to be taught (where you need to go), and the assessment process determines where students are on the content scheduled to be taught next (where you are starting from). In this chapter, you will learn how to reach your destination by planning your instruction so you know what to focus on for students to achieve what they need to learn in the time provided. This process involves translating student assessment data into teacher templates (TTs) and student learning formats (SLFs) using the *Everyone Can* resource materials. Teacher templates and student learning formats are new terms for what has traditionally been called lesson planning. The ABC model uses different terms to highlight the need to focus on both what the teacher and the students need to do during a lesson for learning to occur. We will present this process using the five implementation planning steps.

Few teachers deny the necessity of planning, but few agree on precisely how much planning is needed. Planning at the lesson level must be done individually by each teacher. No two teachers or

> ## Implementation Planning Steps
>
> 1. Set student initial and target learning expectations.
> 2. Identify student learning needs.
> 3. Create instructional groupings based on focal points.
> 4. Select learning activities.
> 5. Design teaching templates and student learning formats.

two classes of students are exactly alike, so different plans are needed to match the strengths and weaknesses of the teacher and the unique needs of the students in the class. That said, teachers do not have to do their planning in isolation. Teachers should be encouraged to share their teaching techniques and to request ideas from other teachers when planning instruction.

Implementation planning is effectively using student assessment data in planning daily instructional activities, games, and conditions to ensure each student's acquisition of the objectives in the program plan. Effective implementation planning enables the teacher to individualize instruction for all students based on their unique needs. The aim of implementation planning is to appropriately structure the learning environment to student ability so that each student is successful in learning.

STEP ❶
SET STUDENT INITIAL AND TARGET LEARNING EXPECTATIONS

The purpose of collecting initial assessment data is to provide teachers with information regarding the instructional needs of their students. This information is then used to make a variety of implementation planning decisions, such as setting student learning expectations, grouping students with common instructional needs, identifying instructional priorities, and selecting appropriate learning activities. The results of these decisions culminate in a plan called a teaching template. To begin this process, the first step is to review and interpret the student assessment data. Figure 3.1 shows a scoresheet for the catch that contains student initial entry assessment data. It can be initially overwhelming to see this array of Xs and Os, but interpretation is simplified by making a series of systematic decisions.

Initial Learning Expectations

The initial decision is to determine which focal point each student needs to work on first, which is done by reviewing each student's initial assessment score and marking the focal point the student is closest to achieving next by shading in the box lightly with a colored pencil. Remember to consider your ACE ratings and to review any comments you made on the scoresheet during assessment. For example, a review of the scoresheet in figure 3.1 reveals that Andrew is trapping the ball between the palms of his hands and not fully using his fingers to control the ball (focal point c). He is also not bending his elbows to retract the arms and help absorb the force of the ball when catching (focal point d). The decision is that with a little instruction this student can learn to flex his fingers and use them when catching the ball. So instruction begins with a focus on catching with the fingers. Because this is the first focal point that Andrew needs to learn for this objective, this box on the scoresheet is shaded in with small dots. When this focal point is achieved, the scoresheet will be updated (i.e., an X placed over the initial O) and then work begun on retracting the arms to absorb force. Figure 3.2 shows a catch scoresheet with the initial learning expectations for each student indicated

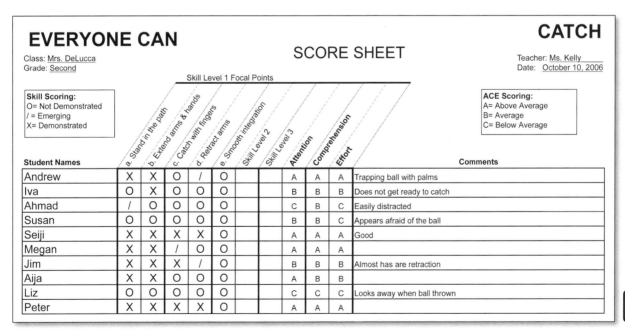

EVERYONE CAN   SCORE SHEET   CATCH

Class: Mrs. DeLucca
Grade: Second

Teacher: Ms. Kelly
Date: October 10, 2006

Skill Level 1 Focal Points

Skill Scoring:
O= Not Demonstrated
/ = Emerging
X= Demonstrated

ACE Scoring:
A= Above Average
B= Average
C= Below Average

Student Names	a. Stand in the path	b. Extend arms & hands	c. Catch with fingers	d. Retract arms	e. Smooth integration	Skill Level 2	Skill Level 3	Attention	Comprehension	Effort	Comments
Andrew	X	X	O	/	O			A	A	A	Trapping ball with palms
Iva	O	X	O	O	O			B	B	B	Does not get ready to catch
Ahmad	/	O	O	O	O			C	B	C	Easily distracted
Susan	O	O	O	O	O			B	B	C	Appears afraid of the ball
Seiji	X	X	X	X	O			A	A	A	Good
Megan	X	X	/	O	O			A	A	A	
Jim	X	X	X	/	O			B	B	B	Almost has are retraction
Aija	X	X	O	O	O			A	B	B	
Liz	O	O	O	O	O			C	C	C	Looks away when ball thrown
Peter	X	X	X	X	O			A	A	A	

Figure 3.1 Catch scoresheet with entry assessment data.

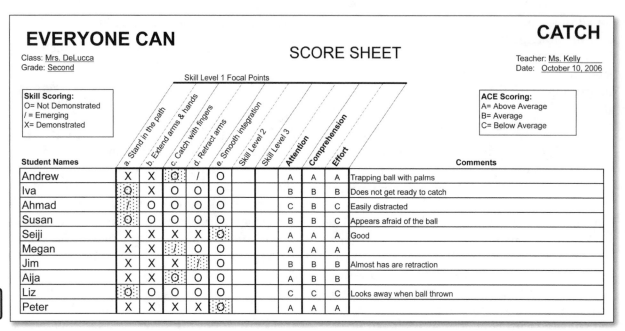

Figure 3.2   Catch scoresheet with initial learning expectations.

by a dotted pattern. Note we have used a dotted background pattern to represent shading in figure 3.2 because it is not in color.

Target Learning Expectations

The next decision to make is how much progress students are expected to make during the current instruction block. Although mastery of all focal points is the ultimate goal, many students require multiple blocks and in many cases multiple years of instruction to achieve some objectives. Target learning expectations are designed to indicate how much progress the teacher expects each student to make during the current theme block. Target learning expectations must be set individually for each student and depend on several considerations:

- How close the student is to achieving the focal points
- The amount of instruction time available
- Characteristics of the focal points (some focal points are learned more easily than others)
- ACE characteristics

- Size of area available and its characteristics
- Equipment suitability and availability
- Number of teachers and teacher aides available
- Ability of students to work in groups
- Level of assistance needed

Target learning expectancies are recorded using the same method used for the initial target expectations except that a different color is used to shade the focal points. Note we have used a different background pattern (i.e., thin lines) in figure 3.3 to represent a different color. Depending on the ability level of the students and the length of the instruction block, it might be common to mark two or more focal points as the target learning expectations for certain students. Review of figure 3.3 reveals that Ahmad, Megan, and Peter have each been targeted to achieve two focal points during this instruction block. Figure 3.3 shows a catch scoresheet with target learning expectations marked with thin vertical lines for each student.

Recording initial and target learning expectations for each student provides a baseline that is important for interpreting student progress and teacher effectiveness (discussed in chapter 5 on

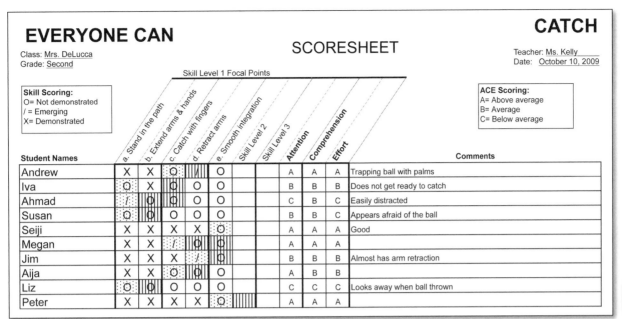

Figure 3.3 Catch scoresheet with target learning expectations.

evaluation). The point to be stressed here is that if you do not record initial and target learning expectations you will have a tough time evaluating student progress and your teaching effectiveness at the conclusion of the instruction block.

STEP ❷
IDENTIFY STUDENT LEARNING NEEDS

In addition to knowing what focal point each student needs to learn first, you must also understand the unique learning needs of each student. All students require and deserve a positive and safe learning environment, but tremendous individual differences exist in the conditions needed for optimal learning for different students. Some students are self-motivated and can work independently with little supervision or prompting. All these students need is a clear understanding of what focal point they need to work on and how to practice it, and they are set. Other students are easily distracted and require a structured learning environment, physical assistance, and significant reinforcement when learning a new skill. During assessment, you recorded information about stu-

dent attention, comprehension, and effort. This information helps you evaluate the validity of the assessment data collected (i.e., was the performance observed an accurate representation of the student's ability?) and identify unique needs that must be addressed when planning an appropriate learning environment for each student.

For students to learn, they must feel secure enough in the learning environment to take a risk. Learning any new task involves the risk of failure. This is particularly true in physical education where performance can be seen by everyone else. For students to learn motor skills, they must want to learn the skill and believe they can learn it. Students who have had success in learning motor skills in the past are usually highly motivated to learn new skills and confident they can learn them. Given their high levels of motivation and confidence, these students can usually endure reasonable amounts of failure during early learning of new skills, which allows them to persevere and perform enough practice trials to eventually learn the skill. Other students, unfortunately, come to physical education with high failure histories in terms of learning motor skills. These students are less motivated and less confident because they see learning new motor skills as a chance to fail again and not as an opportunity to succeed. As a teacher you must assess each student's level of motivation and confidence and plan instruction accordingly.

In addition to knowing what to teach, which was discussed in step 1, and how to teach it, which is discussed in step 4, you must control three critical aspects of the learning environment. These aspects are discussed in the following sections.

Determine Appropriate Level of Assistance

While our goal is to make all our students independent learners, most elementary students require some assistance from the teacher to learn motor skills when they are not performing a skill correctly. Their greatest challenge is understanding what it is they are doing wrong and how to correct it. Your first challenge in the learning environment is to provide them with the appropriate level of assistance while encouraging them to become more independent learners. The key is communicating what needs to be done by the students in a way that is comprehensible to them. Telling students to "almost completely extend your throwing arm while shifting your weight to your back foot" is technically correct, but this instruction might mean nothing to many students. For some students, the most efficient way to communicate is to physically manipulate them to give them a feel of the movement. For other students, a demonstration might do the trick. For still others, a simple visual cue such as

"make a T when you throw" could be the key to communicating. Figure 3.4 shows a continuum of levels of assistance commonly used by teachers. As a rule, start at the level of assistance that ensures students will experience success during early learning. Then gradually fade your assistance.

Have Realistic Learning Expectations

In step 1, we stressed that teachers need to establish initial and target learning expectations for each student when planning instruction. It is also imperative that this information be communicated to the students. Most elementary students lack the experience to set realistic expectations for themselves. If the teacher states that they are going to learn how to skip today, most students take the teacher literally and expect that if they do what the teacher says they will learn to skip that day. Because the skip is a relatively complex locomotor skill, it is likely that many students will not learn this skill in one class period. If realistic expectations are not set for these students, based on their initial assessment data, many might give up after the first class or two and just conclude they cannot skip. A better approach is to inform students that the skip has four focal points and to tell them which ones they have already mastered. They should then be told which component they need to work on next and given some realistic goal of how long it might take them to learn this focal point. All learners want to learn the skills

FIGURE 3.4
Levels of Assistance

Level	Example
Verbal cues	"Follow through."
Verbal instructions	"Step and then hop on the same foot."
Visual prompts	Picture cards or skill posters.
Demonstrations	Teacher or a student shows how to do the skill.
Physical prompts	Student's leg is touched to let him or her know which foot to kick with.
Physical assistance	The underhand roll is done with the student so student gets a feel for the movement.

that are being taught and are constantly looking for information that provides feedback on how they are doing. But if students are not provided with realistic benchmarks to use to evaluate their progress, they are likely to set expectations that are too high (e.g., mastering the skill in one class period) and then subsequently judge themselves as failing when they cannot achieve this expectation.

Provide Feedback

For learning to occur, students must receive timely and accurate feedback. When learning motor skills, there are two categories of feedback: knowledge of performance (KP) and knowledge of results (KR). Knowledge of performance lets the learner know whether focal points of the skill have been executed correctly. Knowledge of results gives the learner information about the outcome of the performance, such as how far the ball was thrown, whether the target was hit, or if the ball went in the basket. During early learning, the most important feedback is knowledge of performance. KP requires the ability to assess performance and give relevant feedback or to design instructional tasks that can provide KP. Initially, both of these tasks must be performed by teachers because they are the only ones who know the focal points of the skills and how to observe them. However, teachers are strongly encouraged to teach their students the focal points of the skills being learned and how to observe them. Once this is done, students can assess and provide feedback to each other. Teachers must also use their knowledge of the focal points of the skills being taught to design instruction activities that provide feedback. For example, foot prints could be used at a throwing station designed to work on weight transfer during the overhand throw. As students are throwing, they can self-evaluate whether they are stepping on the right foot prints with the correct feet.

Unfortunately, during early learning, KR frequently competes with KP and has a negative impact on student learning. If instruction is not designed so that the student receives immediate and meaningful KP, all they receive is KR because it is always present. Consider this example. A student is practicing a basketball set shot. He takes a couple of shots attempting to replicate the demonstration the teacher gave and focusing on the focal points she reviewed. However, after each shot all he knows is that he is consistently shooting the ball short and missing the basket. Based on this feedback, the student decides to try running, jumping, and throwing the ball while shooting to get more power. After doing this a couple of times, one of the shots goes in purely by chance. Given more time to practice, what pattern to you think this student will work on? The one the teacher is trying to teach, or his new run, jump, and throw pattern?

What can we learn from this example? The take-home message is that KR can be very powerful and must be planned for and controlled by the teacher. How can this be done in our example? One way is to alter the task so that KR does not compete with KP. For example, during initial learning we could give the student a smaller, lighter basketball and position him closer to a lower and bigger basket so that the majority of shots he took with the desired shooting pattern had a high probability of going in. We would then gradually increase the distance and decrease the size of the basket as his performance and success increased.

It should be clear now that in addition to knowing which focal point each student needs to work on next for the skill being taught, the teacher must design a safe and positive learning environment that promotes learning. To accomplish this you must be able to assess the learning needs of your students and then provide the appropriate level of assistance, set realistic learning expectations, and control the type of feedback they receive.

STEP ❸
CREATE INSTRUCTIONAL GROUPINGS BASED ON FOCAL POINTS

Now that you have color coded your scoresheet with the initial and target learning expectations and considered the unique learning attributes of your students, use this information to guide the formation of your instructional groupings. Scan down the columns for each of the focal points and skill levels. In a class of 25 students, 10 might have achieved nearly all the focal points in skill level 1, the mature pattern, but need to work on smooth integration, whereas the other 15 might need to practice particular focal points. With this information recorded on the scoresheet, students can be grouped according to their instructional needs. You should also review your ACE ratings and any comments you recorded on your scoresheet while assessing. Some teachers group students with like abilities; others prefer a mixed group of students working on different focal points or different skill levels on the same objective. Social interaction is facilitated by the use of individualized and teacher-directed group instruction. Grouping students with different skill needs, as opposed to homogeneous groupings, may also help promote self-concept and prevent stigmatization that can result when too much attention is focused on students who are different or whose skill functioning is below average. In the mixed ability group (each working on different focal points or skill levels), a team concept has proven effective. The members of the team help each other, and for every focal point gain for the team (i.e., group), a reward is given. Students can be regrouped into teams when different objectives are taught. Whatever grouping pattern is used, it must be tailored to fit the task. Some patterns depend on the class size and number of teacher helpers, if any.

In each grouping, individual differences (i.e., focal points) are identified and assigned to the student to learn. In some instances, performance contracting can be used to individualize instruction and address unique student needs. The student and teacher decide together the focal point to begin to work on and plan activities within the class structure. Subgroups change as students acquire the skills or when the objectives change. As you teach, you will know which students work best in small and large groups, or which ones need more one-to-one instruction in the initial learning stages. Be sure to plan for students to have independence in the teaching-learning situation as they are ready. Give them the opportunity to plan their instruction focused on specific assigned learning tasks. Monitor their activities and help them learn how to learn.

A strength of the *Everyone Can* performance objectives and the scoresheets is that they are designed to measure and organize student performance around the key focal points needed to master each objective in the curriculum. Once initial and target performance expectations are marked on the scoresheet, you can use this information to guide the formation of all types of instructional groupings.

STEP ❹
SELECT LEARNING ACTIVITIES

Now that you know which focal points and skill levels students need to work on, you are ready to begin identifying learning activities. Eight factors should be considered when selecting activities:

1. Skill levels and focal points both needed and already achieved by most students
2. Number of students
3. Number of teachers and aides or volunteers
4. Size of the area available
5. Amount of equipment
6. Instructional groupings
7. Student ACE characteristics
8. Characteristics of the learning environment

With these factors in mind, you are ready to tap into the *Everyone Can* instructional resources. The *Everyone Can* instructional resource materials are organized around the focal points and skill levels of each performance objective. Five types of materials are provided for each objective; they are summarized in table 3.1 and briefly described below.

Teaching Instructional Activities

During initial instruction on many objectives it is not uncommon for the majority of students to need work on the same focal points. For these situations, *Everyone Can* provides two large group instructional activities for each focal point. These are large-group instructional activities that involve the total class. Teachers can use these activities as they are or modify them to create their own activities. The first page of the instructional

Table 3.1   Summary of *Everyone Can* Resource Materials

Everyone Can resource materials	#	Resource description
Teaching instructional activities	1,026	Detailed instruction recommendations on how to teach each focal point of the performance objective.
Station task cards	1,026	These cards are instruction aids to be used by teachers to define instruction stations in their classes designed to focus on focal points of each performance objective.
Games	313	Large- and small-group games are provided for each performance objective and keyed to each focal point of each performance objective.
Posters	70	A visual depiction of the essential focal points and skill levels of the performance objective.
Disability accommodations	70	Guidelines on how teachers can modify each performance objective and instruction to address the unique needs of students with disabilities.

activities for the catch performance objective is shown in figure 3.5. Information is provided on general teaching recommendations as well as specifics on organization, materials, cues, and feedback that can be used when teaching each focal point and skill level of the objective. In addition, each instructional activity is keyed to a number of large- and small-group games that can be used as practice activities once students understand which focal point they are working on correcting.

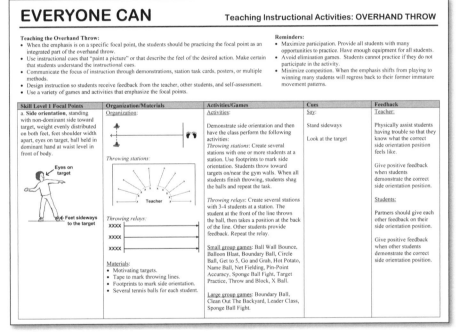

Figure 3.5   Sample teaching instructional activities.

Illustration reprinted from J. Wessel, 1976, *I can: Object control* (North Brook, IL: Hubbard Scientific Company), 35. By permission of J. Wessel.

Station Task Cards

Sometimes when you review class assessment information, you will find that the needs of students are distributed across several of the focal points for the skill being taught. In these situations it might be appropriate to use instruction stations, where each station focuses on a specific focal point of the skill. *Everyone Can* provides two station activities for each focal point designed to

be used by teachers to define and set up instruction stations. A sample station card is shown in figure 3.6. The station cards can be used as they are or can be modified by teachers to create their own stations. Note that each activity on the station card is linked to a number of small-group games that can be used to reinforce and encourage additional practice on focal points once students understand what they need to focus on.

Posters

In both large- and small-group instructional settings, it is sometimes valuable to have pictures of how the skill should be performed readily available so students can refer to the pictures during instruction. *Everyone Can* provides sample posters for each objective that highlight the key focal points of the skills. A sample poster is shown in figure 3.7.

Games

Once students understand which focal points they need to work on for the skill being taught, the next thing they need is lots of practice trials to develop the correct performance of the focal point. One way to get students to practice is to involve them in a game they perceive as fun. As we have mentioned, the large-group instructional

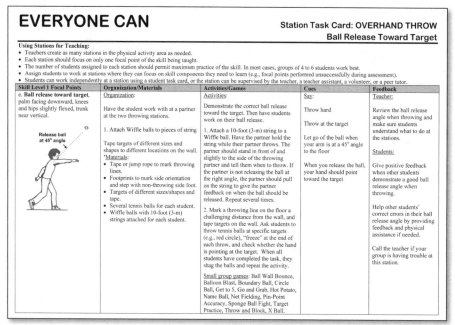

Figure 3.6 Sample station task cards.

Illustration reprinted from J. Wessel, 1976, *I can: Object control* (North Brook, IL: Hubbard Scientific Company), 35. By permission of J. Wessel.

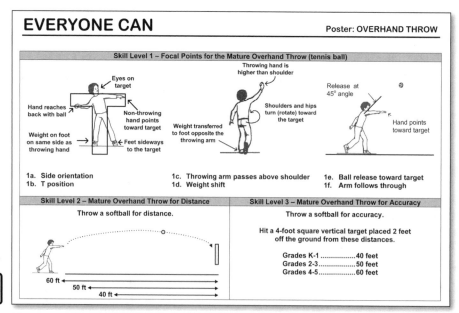

Figure 3.7 Sample poster.

Illustrations reprinted from J. Wessel, 1976, *I can: Object control* (North Brook, IL: Hubbard Scientific Company), 35. By permission of J. Wessel.

activities and the station task cards should be used to teach students how to correctly perform the focal points. To assist in getting them to practice these correct performances, a number of small- and large-group games has been provided in the *Everyone Can* materials for each focal point of each objective. A sample game is shown in figure 3.8. Teachers can use these games as they are or modify them to create their own games. Note that each game has been given a physical activity rating (easy, moderate, or vigorous) so the game can be integrated with the other fitness activities covered in the program.

Disability Accommodations

A challenge for many teachers is knowing how to accommodate students with mild and moderate disabilities who are included in their general physical education program. While using the *Everyone Can* assessing items and designing instruction around their specific needs will assist in this process, a series of general instructional guidelines are provided for teachers to assist them in accommodating the needs of students with developmental, sensory, and physical disabilities for each objective. A sample disability accommodations sheet is shown in figure 3.9.

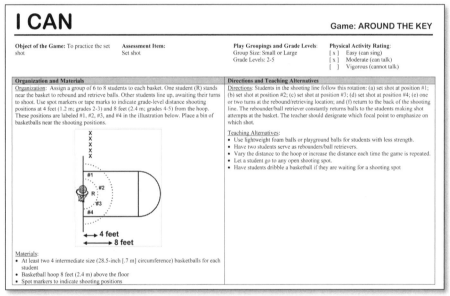

Figure 3.8 Sample game.

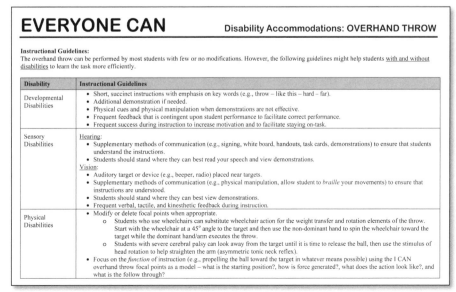

Figure 3.9 Disability accommodations sheet.

STEP ❺
DESIGN TEACHING TEMPLATES AND STUDENT LEARNING FORMATS

At this point in the planning process, you should know which focal point each student needs to focus on and how you want to group your students based on their unique learning needs. You have a wealth of learning activities and games that can be used to address these student needs. Your next step is to organize all this information into an implementation plan—traditionally called a lesson plan. In the ABC model we use two planning documents to define a lesson. The first document is a teaching template, which focuses on what the teacher does during the lesson. The second document is a student learning format, which focuses on what the student does during the lesson. The actual name of the form or whether it is one or two forms does not really matter. What is important is that in your planning you address both your own role and responsibilities as well as those of your students.

Teaching templates define the overall structure of a lesson and are designed to answer five questions:

1. What are the standard managerial procedures?
2. What is the format of the lesson?
3. What content needs to be taught?
4. How will the content be presented and practiced?
5. How will the environment be organized for instruction?

A teaching template may be used for one day or over several class sessions (sometimes with minor revisions). Each template contains a statement of the standard managerial procedures, the format of the lesson, the objectives to be taught, the time to be spent on each objective, the focal point focus of instruction for each objective, instruction cues, learning experiences, organization, equipment, and transition between lesson sections. Figure 3.10 shows a sample teaching template. We recommended creating your teaching templates using a word processor. It is then a simple task to modify the template, such as changing activities or instructional groupings, based on student performance in the previous lesson.

There is nothing sacred about the format of the teaching template. What is important is that it contains the right information and is functional for you to use when you are teaching. Here are some general guidelines to consider when developing your teaching templates:

1. Identify the objectives that need to be addressed and the time allocated for each objective. In most lessons you will be working on several different objectives. You will also need to know the instructional focus for each objective, determined by student assessment data and initial and target learning expectations.

2. Divide your lesson into a logical series of sections and identify the focus of each section. In the ABC model we use Introduction, Lesson Body, and Summary.

    a. Introduction—review, introductions, and warm-up

      • Review the previous lesson.
      • Introduce new or review current objectives being worked on.
      • Explain the focal points and instructional cues that will be focused on in this class.
      • Use both verbal cues and demonstrations.
      • Use physical fitness objectives for warm-up activities.

    b. Lesson Body—Learning experiences, activities, and games

      • Identify how students will be grouped based on their assessment data.
      • Provide time for guided practice with feedback.
      • Plan for application of skills in games and activities that are highly motivating.

    c. Summary—Review the focal points addressed in the lesson, summary activity, and cool-down.

FIGURE 3.10
ABC School District Teaching Template

Grade: First   Class: Ms. Jones   Teacher: J. DeLucca

Start Date: October 20, 2003 End Date: November 26, 2003

Standard Managerial Procedures

See teacher notebook for standard class procedures. When students enter the gym they pick up their individual task cards and immediately go to a carpet square and begin their stretching. Students are allowed to talk until the class begins.

Format	Objectives (Time)	Instructional Focus	Instructional Cue	Learning Experiences	Organization	Equip.	Transition
Intro	Stretching (2) Warm-up (2) Work habits (1)	Static stretching without bouncing	"Reach and hold": sit& reach; hurdlers stretch; standing - bend and hang. "Best Effort"	Teacher directed. Teacher explains which muscles need to be stretched and warmed up before activity. Near the end teacher reviews "Work habits" objective and the focus on "Giving best effort" on all tasks.	Scattered in assigned spaces on carpet squares which are distributed before the class arrives	Carpet squares	End of warm-up students instructed to pickup carpet squares and put in box and then run 2 laps around the gym
Body	Hop (10)	Arm Lift	Use arms to "lift" body when you hop "Step-hop-close"	Demonstrate the correct position and lift of the arms when hopping. Have the students hop around the outside of the gym. On command from the teacher have the students continue hopping while not using their arms and holding them straight along their sides. On the next signal have the students use their arms correctly. Repeat several times and then have the students discuss how the arms help them hop.	Setup a running course around the outside of the gym. Have the students spread out so that they can hop without bumping into other students.	Cones to mark a course around the gym	On a signal from teacher students stop and face the center of the gym for instructions

(continued)

Figure 3.10 (continued)

Format	Objectives (Time)	Instructional Focus	Instructional Cue	Learning Experiences	Organization	Equip.	Transition
	Slide (10)	Period of nonsupport	"Feel" when your feet are both off the ground	Demonstrate that when Sliding there is a period of nonsupport where both feet are temporarily off the ground. Have the students spread out around the course and then practice Sliding making sure they demonstrate a period of nonsupport whenever they Slide over an obstacle. Periodically have the students reverse direction and start their Slide with their other foot.	Use the same course as for the hop and existing lines, tape, or other objects like jump ropes to mark obstacles on the course.	Tape or jump ropes to make low obstacles	
Summary	Hop (3)	Arm Lift	Use arms to "lift" body when you hop "Step-hop-close"	Play "Round the Sun." Explain and demonstrate how to hop/slide the course. The partners should face each other and hold hands. When the game begins, each pair must slide down, go around the cone, slide back, and then tag the next pair on their team. When a team finishes the course they have to sit down. The first team to have all its members complete the course and sitting down wins.	Make several equal sized teams of students paired as partners. Mark a start line for each team and place a cone 50 feet in front of each team.	Cones	Between each round of the game review the focal points and change skills.
	Slide(2)	Period of nonsupport	"Feel" when your feet are both off the ground				

Reflections

54

- Review and demonstrate the focal points that were the focus of the instruction.
- Conduct a large-group activity in which students can apply the skills being learned.
- Finish with a transition activity that allows the students to cool down and calm down.

3. Match the selection of the learning activities to the needs of the students, the nature of the objective, and the learning environment by considering the following factors:

- expectations
- activity level desired (easy, moderate, or vigorous)
- space available
- equipment/availability ratio
- student/teacher ratio
- ability level of the students
- number of dependent and independent learners
- individual/small group/large group
- special needs of students
- levels of assistance
- type and frequency of feedback
- control of success and challenge tasks
- setup and transition time between activities

4. Identify and coordinate the organizational formations needed for the lesson so students can smoothly transition from one formation to another:

a. Formations: circle, line, semicircle, scattered

b. Considerations:
- Visibility of students
- Student familiarity with organization
- Student knowledge of class routines, signals, and transitions

c. Instructional groupings: peers, small groups, team groups, large groups

5. Determine the equipment and space needs for each instructional activity in the lesson:

- Provide enough equipment for each student whenever possible.
- Set up and organize equipment prior to instruction.
- Define and mark boundaries for activities and stations.
- Organize and position equipment in stations to maximize safety.
- Select equipment that maximizes the number of practice trials and minimizes time spent retrieving and setting-up equipment between trials.

6. Transition from one activity to another or from one location to another:

- Use established signals so students know when to stop and when to move.
- Use other objectives (e.g., different locomotor skills) to move between stations and activities to maximize on-task time.
- Use standardized formations so students know where to be.

Student learning formats (SLFs) complement teaching templates and focus on what the students should be doing during instruction. The ABC model presents an SLF as a separate document to highlight the importance of carefully thinking through what students will do during each learning experience. You can incorporate the SLF information into your teaching template if it is easier for you to work with just one document. Figure 3.11 shows a sample SLF. SLFs should be designed to address the following six questions from the perspective of the students:

1. Where should I be?
2. Whom should I be working with?
3. What are my responsibilities during instruction?
4. How do I know if I am being successful?
5. What are the teacher's expectations of me?
6. What should I do if I cannot meet the teacher's expectations or when I do meet them?

FIGURE 3.11
ABC School District Student Learning Format

Grade: First   Class: Ms. Jones   Teacher: J. DeLucca

Start Date: October 20, 2007   End Date: November 26. 2007

Groupings

Keep Dave and Marc in the front during demonstrations. During the game, put Heather, Eunie, Brenan, and Roger on different teams. Keep Bill and Paul apart during group activities and do not put on the same relay team.

Objective(s)	Focus	Cues	Groupings	Expectations	Feedback	Comments
Stretching Warm-up Work habits	Getting ready for activity	"Reach & hold" "Best Effort"	Students on prearranged carpet squares	Do stretches demonstrated by teacher. Understand why muscles need to be stretched and warmed up. Understand to learn students must give their best effort.	Ask questions if you do not understand. Observe other students and give them feedback	After the demonstrations ask the students why it is important to stretch and warm up?
Hop	Arm lift	Use arms to "lift" body when hopping	Large group activity, maintain personal space and respect the personal space of others	Watch teacher demonstration. Hop around gym and on signal from teacher hold arms at sides and on the next signal use them to help you hop.	Ask questions if you do not understand or do not feel a difference when hopping.	Have students go slow and take big hops.
Slide	Period of nonsupport	"Feel" when both feet are off the ground	Large group activity, maintain personal space and respect the personal space of others	Watch teacher demonstration. Slide around gym and slide over objects without touching them. On signal from teacher change directions.	Ask questions if you do not understand or if you do not feel the period of nonsupport when you slide.	Have students increase the size of their step-hops

Objective(s)	Focus	Cues	Groupings	Expectations	Feedback	Comments
Hop & Slide	Arm lift Period of nonsupport	Arm "lift" "Feel" the nonsupport	Relay teams paired with a partner	Hold hands with partner and hop/slide down, around the cone, and back. Tag next pair and then sit down.	Ask questions if you do not understand . Give partner and teams feedback on their hopping and sliding.	Rearrange the teams after each game to make them equal.

Reflections

For young students, these questions must be addressed by the teacher and communicated to the students. For older students, other means can be used to communicate this information, such as using the *Everyone Can* station task cards. The grouping section of the SLF provides a reminder of how students should be grouped. For example, in figure 3.11, Heather, Eunie, Brenan, and Roger are four students who have already mastered the skill level 1 focal points for the hop and the slide, and the teacher wants one of them on each relay team to serve as a model. Also note that the Expectations and Feedback sections communicate to the students specifically what they are supposed to do during each activity. Again, the format of the SLF is not important as long as these questions are addressed in your lesson planning.

Any day-by-day changes made while teaching are written directly on the teaching template or SLFs in the reflection section. These procedures are helpful when reviewing activities and games in terms of which activities and cues worked best for specific students as well as the class in general for specific objectives. This information will be valuable the next time this objective is worked on and will be discussed in more detail in chapter 5 on evaluation.

Once you have created your teaching template and SLF, your last challenge is organizing your teaching materials for maximum efficiency while teaching. There is no magic method for this, but you must have a way to systematically organize your materials so that you can easily review your teaching templates or record changes in student assessment information. A common method is to use a series of notebooks organized by grade and classes. The first notebook is your "main" notebook that serves as your home base and archive for the teaching materials you have used. Your main notebook is divided into three sections: grades, BTLMs, and classes. Let's say you teach grades K-2 in your school, you have four classes per grade, and your YTLM indicates that you have eight theme blocks for each grade. Your notebook would be divided as shown in figure 3.12.

The first document in your main notebook that precedes the grade-level dividers is the scope and sequence chart (step 5 in program planning). The scope and sequence chart indicates which objectives are to be worked on during each grade in the program. At the beginning of each grade level section are several documents specific to that grade level. These documents are the yearly teaching learning map (YTLM), objective assessment items (OAIs), scoresheets, and *Everyone Can* instructional resources. The YTLM indicates how the content for this grade level has been divided into instructional units called block teaching learning maps (BTLMs). The next set of documents is all the OAIs and scoresheets for the objectives targeted for instruction during this grade. The last set of documents is the *Everyone Can* resource materials referenced in the BTLMs, teaching template (TT), and SLFs. If the *Everyone Can* resource materials are cut and pasted into the TT and SLFs, this section is not needed. However, if the resources are just referenced in the TT and the SLFs, then we recommend that a copy of these materials be made and inserted in this section. Figure 3.13 illustrates the table of contents for the main notebook for the first-grade level.

Once you have created a main notebook, you can create your working notebooks that you use during each instruction block. You can use one or more of these working notebooks depending on the number of classes you teach per grade and the amount of information you are comfortable carrying around while teaching. The working notebooks are usually very thin and contain only three to five pages of the essential material you need during teaching (i.e., TT, SLF, scoresheets). The simplest method is to create a working notebook for each class. This method requires many notebooks, but the information you need for each class is easy to find because it is the only information in the notebook. Other methods are to create slightly larger working notebooks for each grade level, with sections for each class, or to create a working notebook for each day, with sections for each class period. At the end of each block, you simply return the current working notebook materials (e.g., TT, SLF, scoresheets) into the main notebook and take the materials for the next block and insert them in your working notebook.

The notebook method is only one example. Use it, or develop another method that works for you. Some teachers prefer to use a clipboard rather than a notebook. Others prefer to store

FIGURE 3.12
Main Notebook Nested Sections:
Grade, Blocks, and Classes

I. Grade K
  A. BTLM 1
    1. Class 1
      a.
      b.
    2. Class 4
  B. BTLM 2
    1. Class 1
      a.
      b.
    2. Class 4
      a.
      b.
  C. BTLM 8
    1. Class 1
      a.
      b.
    2. Class 4

II. Grade 1
  A. BTLM 1
    1. Class 1
      a.
      b.
    2. Class 4
  B. BTLM 2
    1. Class 1
      a.
      b.
    2. Class 4
      a.
      b.
  C. BTLM 8
    1. Class 1
      a.
      b.
    2. Class 4

FIGURE 3.13
Sample Main Notebook
Table of Contents for First Grade

Scope & Sequence

I. First Grade
  A. YTLM for First Grade
  B. All the Objective Assessment Items for First Grade
  C. Score Sheets for all of the First Grade objectives
  D. Everyone CAN resource materials*
    1. BTLM for 1st Block
      a. Class 1
        • TT
        • SLF
        • Score sheets for objectives in this block
      b. Class 2
        • TT
        • SLF
        • Score sheets for objectives in this block
      c. Class 3
        • TT
        • SLF
        • Score sheets for objectives in this block

(continued)

Figure 3.13 *(continued)*

2. BTLM for 2nd Block
   a. Class 1
      - TT
      - SLF
      - Score sheets for objectives in this block
   b. Class 2
      - TT
      - SLF
      - Score sheets for objectives in this block
   c. Class 3
      - TT
      - SLF
      - Score sheets for objectives in this block
   d. (Repeat for BTLMs 3-8)

II. Kindergarten
   A. YTLM for Kindergarten
   B. All the Objective Assessment Items for this grade
   C. Score Sheets for all of this year's objectives
      1. BTLM for 1st Block
         a. Class 1
            - TT
            - SLF
            - Score sheets for objectives in this block
         b. Class 2
            - TT
            - SLF
            - Score sheets for objectives in this block
         c. Class 3
            - TT
            - SLF
            - Score sheets for objectives in this block
      2. BTLM for 2nd Block
         a. Class 1
            - TT
            - SLF
            - Score sheets for objectives in this block
         b. Class 2
            - TT
            - SLF
            - Score sheets for objectives in this block
         c. Class 3
            - TT
            - SLF
            - Score sheets for objectives in this block
         d. (Repeat for BTLMs 3-8)

Add sections for each additional grade.

*The Everyone CAN materials can be copied and included in the notebook or the specific content from the materials can be cut and pasted into your Teaching Templates and Student Learning formats.

their materials in accordion files instead of three-ring binders. You should develop a method that allows you to keep all your materials organized and provides you easy access to your teaching plans and scoresheets.

Of course if you combine the use of the electronic *Everyone Can* materials with using your computer to generate your TT and SLF, you can store the majority of these materials on your hard drive or a flash drive. In this case, you would probably need paper copies only for the working notebooks. We hope in the near future there will be low-cost windows-based PDAs or tablet PCs that physical educators can use during instruction to provide them ready access to the working notebook information electronically.

SUMMARY

Implementation planning is the effective use of student assessment data in planning daily instructional activities, games, and conditions to enhance students' acquisition of curriculum objectives. Effective implementation planning enables teachers to individualize instruction for all children based on the unique needs of each student. When students do not master the same level of achievement in the time available, different performance standards may be specified for different individuals or groups. This is done on the basis of students' initial assessment performance. As the trend toward individualized, self-paced instruction continues, problems inherent in instruction that is group paced and controlled by fixed time schedules for completing units by grades will be reduced or eliminated. Flexible, self-paced instruction designed around recurrent themes should allow students to be placed in the curriculum at an appropriate instructional level in which they are able to succeed and achieve mastery of the objectives being taught.

During the planning process, the importance of knowing where all your students are on the objective you are teaching and how close they are to achieving their next focal point cannot be stressed enough. All students will experience some degree of failure when learning a new skill. The key to teaching is providing the right balance of success and failure. As a general rule, students who have had greater failure histories in physical education require greater success-to-failure ratios than students who have had high success in physical education. For example, many students with disabilities will make only one or two attempts at a new skill and then give up if they have not been successful. The key to controlling success is to plan for a combination of challenge tasks (skills yet to be learned) and mastery tasks (skills already learned) in each lesson. Low-performing students require a greater ratio of mastery tasks to challenge tasks, particularly during the early phases of learning. A second key to controlling success is to plan to give students control over when to alternate between challenge and mastery tasks. Teachers should be aware that if they do not plan to control the challenge and mastery tasks, students will substitute their own behaviors to compensate, many of which may not be desired (e.g., acting out, avoidance).

We encourage you to complete the chapter's enrichment activities to self-evaluate your understanding of the material presented in this chapter. We also recommend that you ask a peer or colleague to evaluate your planning using the implementation planning self-monitoring form. Remember that the purpose of these activities is to give you feedback so you can optimize your planning. These are not intended to be tests, and no one is expected to be perfect. Your goal is to continually improve the effectiveness and efficiency of your implementation planning.

ENRICHMENT ACTIVITIES

These activities are designed to further assist you in understanding the major concepts addressed in the chapter. Most teachers find it beneficial to interact with the content. These activities allow you to experiment with the content and see how it works in practice. They can be done individually or in small groups.

1. Collect or use a scoresheet with previously collected initial assessment data on an *Everyone Can* objective. With a partner, first individually identify what you each feel should be the initial and target expectations for each student in the class. Then compare and discuss your expectations. Did you use the ACE ratings to guide your decisions?

2. Using the scoresheet for the underhand throw (included in the online resource), answer the following questions:

   - If you wanted to form four instructional groups, how would you group these students and why?

   - Assuming you wanted to use stations to work on this objective in your next lesson, what *Everyone Can* materials would you use to address the needs of the four instructional groups identified in part a?

- Identify two large-group games that you could use for this class that would accommodate the ability levels shown on the scoresheet.

3. Select and review one of the *Everyone Can* instructional resources (e.g., instructional activity or station task card) for a given objective and focal point. What can you do to make this resource better? Can you create additional instructional activities or station task cards for this objective? Share your products with your peers.

4. Review the *Everyone Can* small- and large-group games for an objective you are planning to teach. Using the *Everyone Can* game format, create a new large- and small-group game for this objective. Share your games with your peers and ask for feedback. How could you involve children in this process to make your games even better?

5. Using a scoresheet with initial assessment data, create a teaching template and student learning format for the next lesson. Then use the implementation planning monitoring form to evaluate your plans.

6. Identify a parent of an elementary-aged student whom you know. Determine a developmentally appropriate skill that his or her child would be working on and then share with them the *Everyone Can* station cards. What was the reaction? How can you use this information to assist you when you are teaching and working with the parents of your students?

Implementation Planning Monitor Form

Teacher's Name: _____ Date: _____

Have you achieved the implementation planning objectives discussed in this chapter? Use the checklist below to evaluate your teaching templates and student learning formats.
Instructions: Check the appropriate response.

1. Have you completed a scoresheet for every performance objective included in your teaching template? ☐ Yes ☐ No

2. Did you identify an initial learning expectation for each student and record it on the scoresheet? ☐ Yes ☐ No

3. Have you set target learning expectations for each student to be achieved during this block and recorded these values on the scoresheet? ☐ Yes ☐ No

4. Have you selected the focal point(s) for instruction based on . . .

   a. meeting individual needs? ☐ Yes ☐ No

   b. student initial learning expectations? ☐ Yes ☐ No

   c. instructional groupings? ☐ Yes ☐ No

5. When selecting instructional activities, did you consider . . .

   a. skill levels (and focal points) achieved and needed by the students? ☐ Yes ☐ No

   b. number of students? ☐ Yes ☐ No

   c. number of teachers and aides? ☐ Yes ☐ No

   d. size of area available? ☐ Yes ☐ No

   e. amount of equipment? ☐ Yes ☐ No

   f. student ACE ratings? ☐ Yes ☐ No

   g. level of assistance needed by students? ☐ Yes ☐ No

   h. setting realistic learning expectations? ☐ Yes ☐ No

   i. how feedback will be provided? ☐ Yes ☐ No

   j. the balance of success and challenge tasks? ☐ Yes ☐ No

6. Have you written a teaching template and student learning format for today's lesson? ☐ Yes ☐ No

7. Does your teaching template address the following questions:

   a. What are the standard managerial procedures? ☐ Yes ☐ No

   b. What is the format of the lesson? ☐ Yes ☐ No

   c. What content needs to be taught? ☐ Yes ☐ No

   d. How will the content be presented and practiced? ☐ Yes ☐ No

   e. How will the environment be organized for instruction? ☐ Yes ☐ No

8. Does your student learning format/lesson plan address the following questions from the students' perspective:

   a. Where should I be? ☐ Yes ☐ No

   b. Whom should I be working with? ☐ Yes ☐ No

   c. What are my responsibilities during instruction? ☐ Yes ☐ No

   d. How do I know if I am being successful? ☐ Yes ☐ No

   e. What are the teacher's expectations for me? ☐ Yes ☐ No

   f. What should I do if I cannot meet the teacher's expectations or when I do meet them? ☐ Yes ☐ No

9. Does your teaching template and student learning format include activities and organizations that maximize instruction (repetitions and feedback) on the focal point(s) selected for each student? ☐ Yes ☐ No

10. Are the student learning experiences sufficiently outlined in the teaching template so that you could teach from the template next year? ☐ Yes ☐ No

11. Does the teaching template contain an introduction, body, and summary or the equivalent with time definitions? ☐ Yes ☐ No

12. Does the teaching template contain a variety of activities (within or across the objectives) that are sufficient to maintain interest levels? ☐ Yes ☐ No

13. Does the content of the student learning format provide the opportunity for a successful learning experience for each student? ☐ Yes ☐ No

14. What questions, concerns, or problems related to implementation planning do you have?

_____

_____

_____

_____

CHAPTER 4

TEACHING

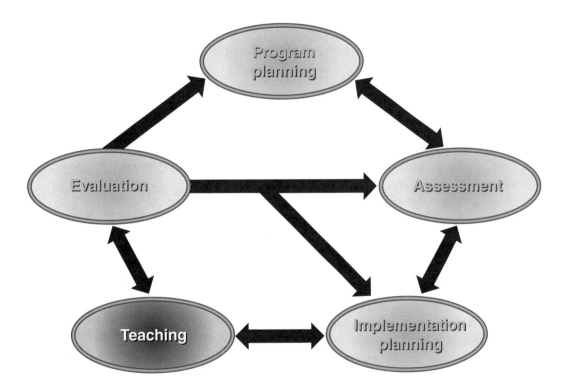

Teaching in the ABC model is defined as managing the learning environment and providing assessment-based instruction so all students achieve mastery of the objectives targeted for instruction. Although presented here as a stand-alone component, teaching is a dynamic process that integrates assessment and implementation planning with the delivery of instruction. Thus, to be an effective teacher you must know what your students need to learn (assessment) and how to effectively address their learning needs. This information has been identified and organized in the teaching template (TT) and student learning formats (SLFs) created during implementation planning. The focus of this chapter is on translating these plans into action.

Teaching is both an art and a science. An effective teacher knows not only what should be done but is able to make it happen.

After reading this chapter, you should be able to . . .

1. Describe how to efficiently organize your instruction materials to facilitate teaching.

2. Identify and explain several techniques that maximize student time spent on tasks related to instructional activities.

3. Define and explain the 12 essential teaching elements.

4. Identify and explain several motivation procedures used to promote student interest in learning.

5. Describe how to use reinforcement and feedback techniques to promote student learning in physical education.

The purpose of this chapter is to highlight essential teaching behaviors required to create a positive learning environment for all students. Much has been written about teaching styles and techniques in elementary methods books. This chapter does not provide an extensive review of this material but instead outlines a series of steps taken to organize and apply these techniques.

Teaching is effectively planning, managing, and instructing a class so that learning occurs for each student. It is the process through which identified educational goals and objectives are achieved through appropriately prescribed activities, enabling each student to receive individualized instruction and to experience success in learning.

Instruction designed to meet individual needs and abilities is the aim of the ABC success cycle. Individualized instruction combines the creativity and resourcefulness of the teacher with the necessary class structure to ensure the objectives targeted for instruction are achieved. To achieve this goal, teachers must first and foremost be organized.

STEP ❶
GET READY

Teacher implementation planning, as described in the previous chapter, is the process of selecting objectives, interpreting students' learning

> ### Teaching Steps
> 1. Get ready.
> 2. Maximize on-task time.
> 3. Apply essential teaching elements.
> 4. Put it all together.

needs based on assessment, selecting appropriate instructional strategies to meet the unique learning needs of each student, and selecting games, drills, and activities that foster the development of the focal points that need to be learned. This information is organized into your TT and SLFs, which are then used to guide the delivery of instruction during the teaching process. In this chapter we focus on preparing to implement the activities or tasks to be presented during class.

Instructional Materials

The first task is to collect and organize all resources needed to teach the lesson. There are many acceptable ways to organize these materials. Develop a way that works for you. A common method is to use a three-ring binder in which the first pages are your TT and SLF for the lesson. Behind these pages you include copies of all the *Everyone Can* resource materials (e.g., instructional activities, station task cards, games) that correspond to the sections of your TT. After organizing these materials, you will need to review them before teaching. Also look for ways that your instruction in physical education can be integrated into the overall curriculum of your students. For example, cues are identified in all the *Everyone Can* instructional materials. It is important to use these cues consistently so students make the connection between the abstract term and the concrete action it represents. Share the words with the students' classroom teachers so the terms can be integrated into instruction such as reading and spelling.

Equipment and Spatial Planning

The equipment is checked for safety and arranged in the learning environment for class activities. Students need to be actively involved in the learning activities. Ideally, equipment should be available for each student to participate; students should not be waiting in lines or sitting on the floor. If students must work in pairs because of limited equipment, each student should have an instructionally relevant assignment: As one student practices a focal point of a skill, the other student observes and provides feedback.

Plan the spatial arrangements in the instructional area and set up all necessary equipment before students arrive. New equipment should be introduced gradually and systematically as students gain target skills. Low-functioning students might need to have distractions removed from the environment during initial instruction. Examine your instruction area in advance and make sure extraneous equipment, materials, and noise are eliminated, or at least minimized as much as possible. It might be helpful to use mats or screens to set off smaller instructional spaces within a larger room. Portable walls provide physical limits for the activity and screen out potentially distracting sights and sounds. These areas may also serve as time-out areas for some students.

Standardized Management Procedures

A universal characteristic among effective teachers is that they have clear and simple rules, signals, routines, and procedures for managing their students. Students generally desire structure and consistency when learning; they want to know where they should be and what they should be doing. Standardized management procedures provide this structure. Class rules and procedures should be written and posted for students. The teacher should review the rules and procedures with students at the beginning of the year. Teachers should follow their own procedures and enforce all rules consistently. When rules are broken, they should be cited by the teacher on a specific basis rather than making general requests for order. Class procedures should focus on what is expected of students during instruction, teacher presentations, drill and practice, and small- or large-group work. Procedures include student behavior before and after instruction, such as beginning the class, getting and putting away equipment, waiting for their turn, and entering and leaving the class. These standardized management procedures should be summarized on the teaching template and periodically reviewed with students as part of instruction.

Organizing Helpers

When available, aides, volunteers, peer-tutors, and other teachers in the physical education setting can be assets. To maximize the benefits, these assistants must be familiar with the established class routines, rules, and procedures. They must also be provided with sufficient training and guidance so they can function independently during instruction. To this end, several instructional resource materials are provided in the *Everyone Can* resources to assist teachers in preparing assistants. Teaching instructional activities and station task cards are provided for every focal point and skill level for each *Everyone Can* objective. Figure 4.1 shows a sample station task card for the T position (focal point b) of the overhand throw. These resources define the focal point and explain how to set up the instruction setting; they also inform assistants what they should do and say while teaching this focal point. Small- and large-group activities and games are also provided for each focal point and skill level for each *Everyone Can* objective. Give these materials to assistants so they know in advance what activities

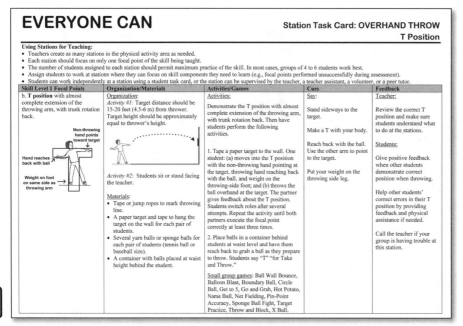

Figure 4.1 Station task card for focal point b of the overhand throw.

Illustrations reprinted from J. Wessel, 1976, *I can: Object control* (North Brook, IL: Hubbard Scientific Company), 35. By permission of J. Wessel.

are involved in a given lesson and how they can help during implementation. Finally, for each *Everyone Can* objective, accommodations are provided for individuals with disabilities. Assistants are frequently asked to help with individuals with disabilities who require various accommodations during instruction in physical education, so this resource is valuable in preparing them to meet the needs of these students. With proper direction, assistants can significantly improve the quality of instruction your students receive.

Planning for Success

The key to teaching is planning in a way that maximizes students' chances for success. Many students have long histories of failure in physical education and with motor skills in general, so they are not highly motivated to work on skills in this area. Thus, it is essential that students not only achieve but that they *perceive* they are achieving during each class, especially early on. Planning for success depends on accurate assessment data, selection of appropriate learning activities, and the use of systematic and explicit feedback. Because someone must always lose (fail) in competitive games, these types of activities should generally be avoided during skill instruction.

Whether students perceive themselves as successful also relates to the standards that pertain. As a rule, if a standard or expectation is not specified by the teacher (e.g., "try to bounce the ball two times using only your fingertips"), students will apply their own standards (e.g., continuously bouncing a ball while moving), commonly based on the ideal or mature performance of the skill. For many students, the ideal performance will be a long-term goal and thus not an appropriate standard for achievement within a single lesson. Teachers must therefore carefully plan instruction so students are given realistic expectations and feedback on their performance. Review your TT and SLFs to make sure you have established ways to communicate clear and attainable performance expectations to your students.

Clarity and Consistency of Instruction

A direct, straightforward method of instruction is recommended when teaching physical and motor skills to students. Instruction should focus on setting clear expectations for students regarding the content, and what specifically they need to do to achieve mastery. This means the teacher must instruct the students in the performance of each objective before expecting them to apply these skills in game situations. The common practice of selecting an activity that involves the target skills (objectives) and assuming students can acquire the skills by simply participating does not work for most students. If and when games are used, their effectiveness as teaching tools is maximized when students know which focal points to work on while playing the game. Table 4.1 summarizes three keys to providing clear and consistent instruction.

Table 4.1 Keys to Delivering Clear and Consistent Instruction

Key	Rationale
Teach the focal points.	This is time well spent because it provides a basis for attending to instruction and self-evaluation during practice. Too often, teachers expect students to deduce these components from demonstrations and random instruction cues (e. g., step with the other foot, point your fingers). For many students attempting to master a new skill, a teacher may employ simple cues such as start position, action, and stop position to facilitate comprehension and encourage skill development. Emphasize the bold phrases highlighted on the objective assessment items and scoresheets. These terms are also highlighted as instruction cues in the *Everyone Can* instruction resource materials.
Use a standardized lesson format.	The ABC model recommends the following lesson format: introduction, lesson body, and summary. Most students respond positively to highly structured and consistent environments. Given this knowledge, teachers should attempt to provide a structured environment to facilitate skill acquisition, particularly during early learning. Standardized procedures such as formations and rules are also recommended to minimize confusion and more easily allow students the opportunity to exhibit self-control. Skill demonstrations, for example, may always be given with the students arranged in an established formation (in a semicircle, on prearranged spots or carpet squares, etc.) that the students know to get in whenever they are told "class demonstration." For practice periods, the gym or classroom may be divided into established stations that focus on the focal points of the skill being taught, thereby minimizing confusion or uncertainty that might interfere with instruction and student learning.
Use simple rules and signals.	The best rules are simple rules that can be easily remembered by students. In addition to the rule, students must know the consequences for not following the rules. It is the teacher's responsibility to ensure rules are consistently followed and enforced. Signals should also be established and consistently enforced to maintain class management. Signals should be kept simple and few in number. For example, to start you need only two signals. A signal that means stop and listen and another that means go to work.

STEP ❷
MAXIMIZE ON-TASK TIME

On-task time refers to the amount of time students spend working on the objectives being taught during instruction. Although on-task time is important in all learning environments, it is particularly important in physical education because of the nature of the instructional environment and the limited amount of time available. In many physical education programs, on-task time can be as low as 10 to 15 percent when the focus is on playing games to teach objectives (e.g., playing kickball to learn how to run, throw, kick, and catch) rather than teaching and practicing specific focal points of objectives. Given that many students typically receive only 36 hours (36 weeks × 2 days per week × 30 minutes per day) of physical education instruction in a year, 10 percent on-task time means that students work on instructional objectives in physical education only 3.6 hours for the year. This obviously is not enough time to develop the muscular strength and coordination needed to learn motor skills or to develop physical fitness. Teachers must thus plan to optimize on-task time in physical education if they truly want their students to develop motor skills.

Maximizing on-task time throughout a lesson is important if each student is to achieve his or her expected gain. Figure 4.2 summarizes practices teachers have identified to increase on-task time. Review these and try to incorporate them into your teaching.

Instruction time should be treated as a valuable resource. At least 60 percent of the student's physical education time should be spent on task with the student physically engaged in learning a specific focal point for the skill being taught. The teacher plans, organizes, and sets up the equipment for the lesson before the class comes to physical education. The class begins and ends promptly. Students move quickly from one activity to another on a signal from the teacher.

FIGURE 4.2
Techniques for Increasing On-Task Time

• Employ a high degree of class structure and good organization. The less time spent on class management and addressing discipline problems, the more time there is for instruction and practice.

• How each minute of available instruction time will be used in a lesson must be carefully considered and planned before a class begins so maximum on-task time is achieved. Teachers, for example, often forget time for transitions between activities; they must be smooth and automatic with little disruption or student off-task behavior. For example, students could practice select locomotor skills while moving between instruction stations.

• Designate a spot in the room for the activity and bring students to that spot before beginning the activity. You might want to establish a routine of beginning every lesson in the same location or in the same formation such as a circle.

• Choose your area(s) for each activity and set up all necessary equipment before the students arrive for the lesson. Provide enough equipment so students do not have to wait around to use it. Do not clutter the space with equipment that is not to be used in the lesson.

• Orient students to the basic instruction in each formation you will use in teaching the objective: for example, teams, circles, lines, relays, scattered.

• Place yourself in a position to continually observe, monitor, and reinforce the performance of students. Make sure all students can see and hear the presentation. Refrain from interrupting student activity with irrelevant or incidental information or dwelling on a topic beyond what is necessary for student understanding.

• The space allocation for each activity area should be clearly defined by markings on the floor. Smaller space areas can be used to eliminate distractions if needed for some students. Use mats, screens, or movable partitions to separate teaching areas. This is another way to define the boundaries of activities or stations as well as for time-out areas.

• Using signals for stop and go is an important classroom procedure to maximize on-task time that should be taught in orientation. Your signals should be consistent and clearly differentiated. For example, "Go" might always be the signal for start and whistle always the signal for stop.

• Give each student several consecutive trials (5 to 10 or more, depending on nature of skill) in a row. For many skills it requires several trials to get the feel for a new movement, which is hard to get if a student is only given one practice trial and then must wait for their next turn.

• Vary stations for practicing different skills.

• Plan lessons so students who are able to practice independently on certain skills are working on them while the teacher assists small groups of students.

• Begin with skills the student can do quickly and easily; move to more difficult items gradually.

• Have students practice as partners with other students whenever possible and appropriate. Pair older or higher skilled students with younger or less-skilled students. Use student assistants from another classroom or another school (e.g., local junior or senior high school). Make sure each partner knows their assigned responsibility.

• Maximize equipment-to-student ratio whenever possible by making homemade equipment (e.g., paper balls; yarn balls; carpet squares; rubber car mats; foam rubber, carpet, or contact paper footprints; pictures or clown faces for targets; empty drum barrels; etc.).

• Select skills and activities that serve as "double payoff" (i.e., two objectives are being learned or practiced at the same time); for example, teaching the focal points of the fundamental skill "run" while students are also running for the health/fitness skill of cardiorespiratory endurance.

• To encourage increasing repetitions of an activity, count the repetitions aloud and have students do one more each time (i.e., say, "You did four . . . now do five").

• Plan game activities so students are not eliminated entirely when they "get out." For example, in a circle game when one student is out, have the student sit in the middle of the circle. When the next student "gets out," have that student take the place of the one in the middle. In this way students get a chance to come back into the game and get more practice time.

• Keep activities short to begin (e.g., 3 to 5 minutes) and gradually increase duration over time. Change size of groups and members of groups to match the ability level of the students and maximize the number of practice trials.

• Use activities or games that accommodate student functioning at various skill levels. Use a more highly skilled student as a model for the rest of the group, or pair skilled and unskilled students.

• Plan instruction around the focal points of objectives being taught. Select drills and activities that involve high participation of all students.

• Modify equipment or set up instruction stations to maximize practice and reduce off-task time. Throwing, for example, can be practiced with paper balls, which can be made in great numbers, do not travel far, and will not roll when they land on the floor. Using paper balls allows this activity to be practiced safely in a small area and enhances repetitive practice by reducing the amount of time required to chase down and collect balls.

The teacher plans the activities and the space requirement so students move to new areas or a new activity with little disruption or time lost. Some teachers mark activity areas or use mats, screens, or markings on the floor to separate activities. Simple signals are established and used consistently.

STEP ❸
APPLY ESSENTIAL TEACHING ELEMENTS

Because the ABC model emphasizes individualizing instruction and teaching the focal points of skills, teachers sometimes think this means students should be lined up and taught one at a time to robotically perform the focal points of each skill. That is a misconception. A structured lesson in the ABC model means that the lesson is objective directed. Skills to be taught are specified by sequential instructional objectives as defined in the *Everyone Can* objective assessment items. Students are assessed on instructional objectives, and specific learning tasks are assigned. Instructional activities and games are tied to specific learning tasks prescribed for the students. Instructional

objectives and prescribed activities are modified to meet each student's needs as he or she progresses toward developing a mature pattern. Using this model, the effective teacher expects high achievement from all students, regardless of their initial ability levels. The teacher takes responsibility for student learning, monitors the class and students' work, and holds students accountable for their work and behaviors. The assessment results are reported to students in simple, clear language to help them understand and make improvement. The teacher runs a goal-directed and orderly class focused on students' needs and interests. To help teachers accomplish this mission, the ABC model identifies 12 essential teaching elements to employ when teaching. We will briefly summarize each of these elements.

Teach to the Objective

Students must know which skill they are learning and which focal points they should be concentrating on each time they perform the skill. Informing each student what he or she needs to work on during a lesson allows the teacher to involve a wide range of ability levels in the same activities while still individualizing instruction.

Select the Correct Level of Difficulty

Ideally, a teacher should always know at what level to design activities for their students. However, when working on new skills, this is not always possible to predict. In these situations, it is best to start at the lowest skill level and with simple activities and then work up to more difficult levels. This ensures that students start out being successful. This procedure is preferable to starting with the highest skill level and allowing students to repeatedly fail until the problem is detected and the activity modified accordingly.

Model Skills

Modeling has been shown to be one of the most effective methods for teaching physical and motor skills. Modeling is sometimes narrowly defined as giving correct demonstrations of desired behaviors during instruction. In physical education, the definition includes continuous modeling of desired fitness, motor skill behaviors, and attitudes. For example, demonstrating how to correctly perform a curl-up is important during instruction of this skill, but it is equally important to regularly model the skill. In this way, students see that the skill must be performed by each person (including the teacher) if one hopes to maintain one's abdominal strength and endurance. This is not to imply that every teacher must be an expert in all motor skills being taught. In fact, in many cases teachers might use a deficit in their own performance as a model and ask the class to help them improve during instruction. Done properly, this can be an extremely powerful motivator for students.

Physically Manipulate the Student's Movements

Effective modeling depends on learners accurately comparing their performances to a visual image of a desired pattern. But many students find it hard to accurately evaluate their own performances after seeing a demonstration. When shown demonstrations of correct and incorrect patterns of a skill, students might insist that their pattern is correct when it is not. Often it works better to communicate a desired set of movements by physically manipulating the student's body, guiding him or her through the pattern. The best way to teach motor skills to many students is to combine physical manipulation with a few carefully selected action words, such as reach, step, and throw.

Explain Relevance

The purpose for learning many fundamental motor skills is not immediately evident to many students. To help motivate them to want to learn these skills, the teacher must explain why and how these skills will be used to perform other, more complex motor behaviors. Teachers must also explain and encourage students to transfer the skills they are learning in physical education to recreational activities outside of school. Given that it can take thousands of practice trials to learn a specific motor skill and that there is probably not enough time to do all of these practice trials during physical education class, students must be encouraged to practice and use their motor skills outside of school. To help students with disabilities, teachers might have to look into recreational opportunities available after school and on weekends and then encourage students to participate in these programs.

Motivate Students

Students need to perceive that they need what is being taught and that chances are good they can learn it. Thus, the teacher must explain why learning the skill is important and structure learning activities so that students experience success. Teachers should ensure that learning tasks are consistent with the messages being given their students. If a teacher tells students that everyone will be able to learn a given skill easily, then students should *all* achieve success in the next activity involving this skill. If students experience failure, this knowledge of their performance (KP) will outweigh the verbal information provided by the teacher. Self-paced and self-reinforcing activities are recommended to keep students' motivation high and to allow the teacher to move freely between stations. Suspending a tambourine against a wall as a target and marking lines on the floor every 2 feet (.6 m) from the target is an example of a self-rewarding and self-paced activity for throwing. Students are instructed to start at the first line (e.g., 6 feet [1.8 m] from the target) and to throw balls (focusing on a specific focal point that needs work) until they hit the target three times in a row. Then they move back to the next line (e.g., 8 feet [2 m]) and throw from that distance until they hit the target three times. This procedure is repeated until they reach the distance at which practice is needed (where they cannot hit the target consistently three times in a row). Targets that make noise can be very effective for students, as long as the teacher can tolerate the noise in the environment. Remember when working on skill level 1 that the size of the target should be increased so that knowledge of results (KR) does not compete with knowledge of performance (KP).

Insist on Active Participation

Students cannot learn motor skills by just watching or listening. Most motor skills require hundreds if not thousands of practice trials to develop. Instruction must be planned and implemented that focuses on the specific focal points that students need to work on and provides them with the maximum amount of time possible to practice these patterns.

Monitor and Adjust Learning

The true skill of teaching is controlling the balance between success and failure. All students will experience some degree of failure when learning a new skill; the key to learning is providing the right balance of success and failure. As a rule, students who have had greater failure histories in physical education need a higher success-to-failure ratio than do students who have had high success histories in physical education. For example, many students with disabilities will try a new skill only once or twice and then give up if they have no success. The key to controlling success is to use a combination of challenge tasks (skills yet to be learned) and mastery tasks (skills already learned). Low-performing students require a greater ratio of mastery tasks to challenge tasks during initial learning. A second key to controlling success is to give students control over when to alternate between challenge and mastery tasks. Teachers should be aware that if they do not control the

challenge and mastery tasks, students will substitute their own behaviors to compensate.

Give Students Some Control

Although teachers should do everything they can to match the demands of instruction tasks to the assessed needs of their students, this can be very challenging when there is one teacher and 30 students. One way to fine-tune these decisions and increase student engagement in instruction is to give some of the control to the students in the form of giving them choices. These choices can range from simple options such as deciding the order in which they want to complete a sequence of stations to problem-solving activities in which students create stations that work on specific focal points. Of course for this to work efficiently, teachers must develop decision-making skills in their students and provide sufficient guidance so all students are actively engaged in this process.

Provide Valuable Reinforcement

As a rule, general positive statements such as "good job, class" provide no instructional information to the students and reinforce as many students for doing something right as they do students who just did something wrong. For positive reinforcement statements to have value, they must be perceived as meaningful by the recipients. Thus we recommend that all reinforcement statements be explicit and instructionally relevant. A good procedure for providing effective feedback in physical education is to break instruction statements into four parts:

1. Say the student's name.
2. State a focal point the student performed correctly.
3. Suggest a focal point–based correction.
4. State a performance criterion.

Here is an example of such feedback: "Mary, that was nice arm extension. Now let's concentrate on that big step on the next three throws." Reinforcement should be systematically distributed so all students receive equal amounts of feedback. If the teacher does not consciously ensure that all students are observed and given some form of positive reinforcement each class, some students might receive a lot of reinforcement and other students receive none. Students should also be provided with a means of monitoring their progress. Posters, to be mounted on gym walls, are provided for each *Everyone Can* objective to illustrate the focal points of the skill being taught. Each time students achieve a component, they can be given a sticker to put on the class chart, or small individual posters can be printed for each student. This form of progress chart focuses the student's attention on the focal points of the skill and provides the teacher with a continuous record of progress. Table 4.2 reviews other common reinforcement and behavior-management techniques that teachers should be familiar with when teaching.

Ensure Lessons Have Closure

Summarize and reinforce what has been learned. Students need accurate feedback on how they have been performing and how a given lesson went. Many times, even when a lesson has been a total disaster, the teacher concludes the lesson telling all students they did a great job. This sends a confusing message to students who just spent most of their time failing or avoiding. The message is that the teacher thinks what they did was okay, and thus the teacher is probably going to do the same thing the next class. If students just failed for an entire period, how motivated do you think they are going to be at the beginning of the next class? On the other hand, if a class does not go well, the teacher should state that and ask students for input on how the next class could be better. This technique gives students some ownership in the class and provides hope that the next class will be better.

Review and Practice to Maintain Skills

After initial instruction on performance objectives, time must be scheduled to periodically review and practice these skills so they are maintained. This is particularly true for maintaining fitness levels. Although students might remember how to perform a correct curl-up several months after learning the skill, they will not be able to maintain the strength (number of curl-ups they could perform at the end of a fitness unit) if they do not regularly practice doing that number. Retention activities can be easily worked into warm-up and summary activities. When a retention activity is implemented, the teacher should review both the focal points and how students could be using the skill outside of physical education.

STEP ❹ PUT IT ALL TOGETHER

Teaching is defined as the management of the instructional environment so that desired learning outcomes are achieved. Inherent in this definition of teaching is a need for instructional control of students and a plan to achieve desired changes in behavior. We have reviewed many teaching concepts and techniques in this chapter. At this point you might feel overwhelmed by all the information and wonder how you are going to maximize on-task time, control success and failure, give students specific instruction cues, and incorporate the 12 essential teaching elements into your teaching. The key is to keep things simple and not try to change all your teaching behaviors at once. Ask yourself, What do my students need to know to learn the skill I am about to teach them?

They need to know . . .

- the focal points of the skill to be taught,
- which focal points they can already execute correctly,
- which focal points they should work on and what to change, and
- how to know when they are being successful.

Now you need to ask yourself what you can do to help your students address these needs. Table 4.3 (p. 77) lists a series of suggestions for ways to get started. Remember: You do not have to take all these suggestions right away. Maybe some of them are already part of your normal teaching routine, or maybe not. Either way, pick two or three and try to work them into your everyday teaching routine. Once you have integrated these behaviors into your teaching, add a couple more.

Table 4.2 Common Reinforcement and Behavior Management Techniques

Procedure	Definition	Use	Example
Positive reinforcement	The feedback of a consequence following the performance of a desired behavior (e.g., learning a skill, or personal-social learning task). Positive reinforcers must be pleasurable to the student receiving them.	To increase the frequency of a desired behavior, use a positive reinforcer, such as social privileges or concrete rewards. Rely on natural consequences of the environment.	The instructor wants to increase the frequency of a student's participation in group games. The student responds well to praise, so every time the student participates in group activities, the teacher praises the student; or every other time the student participates, the teacher tells her how well she is performing. Verbal, pat on the back, handshake, or choose activities the student prefers.
Positive reinforcement schedule	How often a person is reinforced following the performance of the desired behavior.	Continuous reinforcement following every desired behavior results in a very rapid initial increase in the desired behavior, but when the reinforcing is stopped, the behavior drops off quickly. Good for starting children on a new behavior. Intermittent reinforcement is when you do not reinforce every desired behavior. This results in better behavior over a longer period of time.	The instructor wants to increase the frequency of Bill coming to class. Initially he praises Bill every time he comes to class. After 2 weeks the instructor praises Bill every other time he comes to class.
Reinforcing incompatible behaviors	Positively reinforcing behaviors that cannot take place at the same time that an undesirable behavior takes place.	For decreasing the frequency of an undesirable behavior, the instructor must identify behaviors that compete with the undesirable behavior.	Jill occasionally exhibits the undesirable behavior of pushing while waiting in a relay line. The instructor positively reinforces Jill when she stands with her hands to her sides in line. Pushing and standing with hands to the sides cannot take place at the same time.
Modeling	Imitating or demonstrating the component of the skill or the entire skill to provide the student with a visual concept of the desired pattern.	Best used for visual learners or low-level performers and to enhance initial learning of a skill.	The objective for the student(s) is the run. Model the mature pattern emphasizing the proper arm action and the period of nonsupport.
Extinction	The process of withholding reinforcement following the performance of a certain behavior.	A strategy to decrease disruptive behaviors when you have full control of the consequences and when the behavior must not be stopped immediately. After a continuous reinforcement schedule, extinction is rapid. Following an intermittent reinforcement schedule, extinction is gradual.	A student in class is reinforced by the instructor's attention. The student continually complains about everything. The instructor decides to use extinction by planning to ignore the student whenever he complains and giving him more attention when he does not complain.

(continued)

Table 4.2   *(continued)*

Procedure	Definition	Use	Example
Feedback	Providing the student with precise concrete information concerning performance as it relates to the demands of the task.	To increase the rate of learning as well as the level of learning reached. The more specific the knowledge, the more rapidly the skill improves. The longer the delay in giving this feedback, the less effect it has on learning.	The objective for the student is the overhand throw. The student performs several trials while the teacher, aide, volunteer, or peer partner observes. On completion of throws, the teacher says, "Good. You had nice arm extension; now make sure you step on the opposite foot when you throw." Demonstrate stepping on the opposite foot.
Prompting	Providing additional cues or stimuli to help a student perform a skill. The continuum of prompts goes from physical assistance to verbal cues.	For students exhibiting varying ability levels and for complex skills.	The objective selected for the student(s) is the overhand throw. Several students perform well enough that they do not need prompting. Several students need a verbal cue such as "Step on the other foot," while still others need physical assistance in the form of the instructor touching the correct foot to step on.
Physical assists	Manipulating a student's body through part of or an entire motion.	Designed to give the student a feel for the movement.	Touch or tap correct body part to be used. Apply continuous pressure to guide student through the movement.
Demonstration	Teacher, aide, or peer model demonstrates all or part of the behavior desired.	Provides the student with a visual image of the performance.	Demonstrate the skip or demonstrate only the correct arm movement of the skip.
Gestural	The teacher points directly to or in the direction of a stimulus.	Provides additional information to assist the student in performing the skill.	Point to a spot where the student's next step should be while performing a dance.
Verbal	The teacher provides verbal instruction or encouragement to the student.	Provides the student with an auditory cue to assist in performance.	Use *Everyone Can* instruction cues to give specific verbal instruction. such as "Leg up" or "Point your toes."
Fading	The gradual elimination of reinforcers or cues.	To decrease student's dependency on prompts in a gradual manner as the student progresses in ability.	The objective selected for a student is catching. Fade complete physical assistance to partial physical assistance to a verbal cue to no cue or assistance as student progresses in ability.

Table 4.3 Simple Changes You Can Make to Your Teaching

Change	Rationale
1. Teach to the objective	Student and teacher should both know the objectives of the lesson and the focal points that must be demonstrated to perform the skill.
2. Teach the instructional sequence	Students should know the sequence and specifically what they need to do to correct or change their performance on each focal point they are working on.
3. Set clear expectations	Students should understand how many times they may need to practice a skill before they see a significant change in their performance.
4. Practice and relevance	Use adequate, systematic practice and drill time within the lessons and for retention over time. Use a variety of concrete examples of situations in which the skill is performed to accomplish specific outcomes.
5. Feedback	Develop a systematic process to monitor, adjust instruction, and reinforce student work and to correct student errors; positive encouragement through reinforcement is the name of the game.
6. Set clear and explicit rules	Clearly present and spell out the rules and consequences; have students verbalize and demonstrate that they understand.
7. Fade assistance	Gradually fade the level of assistance provided during instruction from physical manipulation to cues inherent in the skill.
8. Review	Use cumulative review at end of each lesson and end of the block that is an accurate reflection of how well the lessons went.
9. Level of difficulty	Use learning activities and games at appropriate levels of difficulty; systematically break larger tasks into smaller components as needed; adapting or modifying.
10. Individualize group instruction	Use individualized, directed group instruction; students working on same objective for individual learning tasks assigned.
11. Independence	Gradually fade from highly teacher-directed activities toward independent work, particularly when problem solving is involved.
12. On-task time	Use effective practices to maximize instruction time available (increase time on task). These should be planned and implemented accordingly prior to, during, and at the end of the lesson.
13. Explicit instruction	Use explicit instruction that informs the students of what they are doing correctly, what they need to focus on next, and performance criteria for the next attempts.

SUMMARY

Good teaching involves effectively managing a learning environment so that desired student learning occurs. For this to happen, the teacher must have the class under instructional control (i.e., must have standardized management procedures in place), know what each student needs to learn for the objectives targeted for instruction (assessment), have a plan to address these needs (have an idea for implementation using the *Everyone Can* resource materials) and, finally, be able to actively engage students in learning the content. As we mentioned at the beginning of the chapter, teaching is both an art and a science. Simply knowing what should be done when teaching is not enough. An effective teacher has a carefully thought-out plan, but he or she must also constantly evaluate and change the plan to meet the ever-changing learning needs of their students. Teaching is a dynamic process. Part of teaching involves careful and thorough planning, but effective teaching can be mastered only through practice, experience, hard work, and meaningful feedback.

We recommend completing the chapter's enrichment activities to self-evaluate your understanding of the material presented. We also encourage you to ask a peer or colleague to evaluate your teaching using the self-monitoring form at the end of this chapter.

ENRICHMENT ACTIVITIES

These activities should help you apply the content you learned in the chapter. Most teachers find it beneficial to interact with the content. These activities allow you to experiment with the content and see how it works in practice.

1. Ask a peer or colleague to observe you teaching a lesson. After the lesson, review the teaching self-monitoring form with your colleague and identify three things you did well and three areas in which you could improve. Provide the observer with the following materials:

   - A copy of your teaching template and student learning formats (i.e., lesson plan)

   - A copy of the instruction materials (e.g., *Everyone Can* instructional activities, station task cards, games, etc.) that complement your teaching template

   - A copy of the scoresheet with preassessment data and initial and target expectations for each student

   - A copy of the teaching self-monitoring form

2. Identify a teacher who is generally perceived to be highly effective and evaluate him or her using the self-monitoring form. How did the teacher do? What are this teacher's strengths? In what areas might this teacher improve?

3. Video one of your lessons. Estimate what you think the on-task time will be for a typical student during your lesson, and write this value down (e.g., 35 percent). Then randomly select one student from your class list. Watch the video and calculate the amount of time this student is on task by (1) using a stopwatch and recording only when the student spends time either attending to instruction or actually performing the objectives identified for instruction in your teaching template; (2) at the end of the lesson, converting the time on the watch to seconds (i.e., $60 \times$ the number of minutes + the remaining seconds); and (3) dividing the value obtained in step 2 by the total length of the class in seconds (e.g., a 30-minute class = 1,800 seconds). Compare your actual on-task time with the estimate you made before you watched the tape. How did you do? What are some ways you could increase your on-task time for the next lesson?

4. At the end of one of your lessons, talk informally with one or two of your students and ask them the questions below. Ask these questions in an informal, positive, and conversational manner. Do not question the answers the students provide or try to justify what you did. Just listen and learn and then thank the students for their input. Questions for the students:

   - What specifically were you trying to learn today?

   - How much progress did you make today, and how do you know you made progress?

   - What part of class did you like the most and why?

   - What part of class did you like the least and why?

Reflect on the students' responses and compare them with your perceptions of how your lesson went. Based on this information, what will you change for the next class? Record these changes on your teaching template.

Teaching Self-Monitor Form

Teacher's name: _____   Date: _____

Have you achieved the teaching objectives posed at the beginning of this chapter? Use the checklist below to evaluate your teaching. Check the appropriate response.

1. Was your teaching template and student learning format implemented as planned? If no, why not?　☐ Yes　☐ No

2. Did the learning activities focus on the objectives and the specific focal point needs identified for the students in this class?　☐ Yes　☐ No

3. Did all of the games optimally involve the objectives and focal points being focused on in this lesson?　☐ Yes　☐ No

4. Were strategies used that corresponded to the identified learning preferences of individual students (styles, modes)?　☐ Yes　☐ No

5. Was it evident that student instructional groupings were based on assessed needs?　☐ Yes　☐ No

6. Did setting up equipment occupy only a minimal amount of your lesson time?　☐ Yes　☐ No

7. Did assistants effectively complete their assigned tasks?　☐ Yes　☐ No

8. Was there a minimal amount of time used to move students from one organization to another during the class period?　☐ Yes　☐ No

9. Were students on task working on prescribed focal points at least 60 percent of the class time?　☐ Yes　☐ No

10. Were concrete examples provided of the skill being taught by using a demonstration (teacher or peer modeling) of the desired performance?　☐ Yes　☐ No

11. Were focal points taught in the manner prescribed in the teaching template?　☐ Yes　☐ No

12. Were instructional/organizational procedures used that allowed students to practice many repetitions of the particular skill (focal point) taught?　☐ Yes　☐ No

13. Were students provided a means of receiving instructionally relevant feedback after each trial as they were performing?　☐ Yes　☐ No

14. Were students provided with the opportunity (where appropriate) for independent decision making (self-direction) during instruction?　☐ Yes　☐ No

15. Were your student reinforcement techniques explicit and positive?　☐ Yes　☐ No

16. Were activities and games structured or modified to maximize student participation time and practice?　☐ Yes　☐ No

17. Did you have a method for you or the students to record performance gains?　☐ Yes　☐ No

18. Do you know that most students enjoyed and experienced success during the learning activities?　☐ Yes　☐ No

CHAPTER **5**

EVALUATION

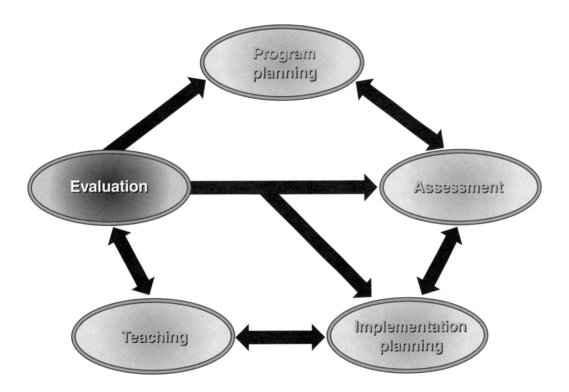

Evaluation is the process of determining whether students are learning the objectives targeted for instruction and if the program is achieving its goals. In the ABC model, evaluation is addressed at two levels: student and program. When some teachers and students hear the term "evaluation," they think it means grading.

Although grading is one aspect of student evaluation, you will learn in this chapter that evaluation encompasses much more than that. Review of the ABC success cycle reveals that evaluation informs all other components in the model. This highlights the significance of evaluation in the overall implementation of the ABC model.

CHAPTER OBJECTIVES

After reading this chapter, you should be able to . . .

1. Explain the purpose and processes involved in student evaluation.
2. Explain the relation between student evaluation and grading.
3. Describe methods for reporting student progress and the program's effectiveness.
4. Distinguish between formative and summative evaluation.
5. Explain the purpose and processes involved in program evaluation.
6. Identify program-adjustment options available based on evaluation findings.

Although evaluation is essential to ensure that a physical education program is being implemented as intended and that students are achieving the objectives targeted for instruction on schedule, little evaluation is typically done in physical education. Do not misinterpret this as meaning evaluation is not important. One of the major reasons evaluation is not performed in many programs is that teachers simply have no data to evaluate. For example, how would you determine if the amount of time spent on teaching kicking to a given grade level this year was sufficient for the students to learn this skill and stay on track with the curriculum? What data is needed to answer this question? Well, you need to know how much time was spent on this objective this year and how much progress students made. In the ABC model, the amount of time allocated for this objective is included in the program plan. The amount of time spent can be calculated from the block teaching learning maps (BTLMs; see chapter 1) and the teacher templates (TT; see chapter 3). Student progress on the kick can be calculated by analyzing the student entry and exit status on the scoresheet for this objective. With these data, you can determine if enough time remains in the program for students to achieve this objective. Of course you need a program plan and student assessment data to be able to determine such matters. This chapter is designed to assist you in organizing your data and give you step-by-step procedures for performing student and program evaluation.

Evaluation Steps

1. Collect reassessment data.
2. Calculate, interpret, and report student performance.
3. Evaluate and grade students' progress.
4. Evaluate your program.
5. Use technology to aid in evaluation.
6. Establish program accountability and justification.

As shown in the in the ABC success cycle, the purpose of evaluation is to determine whether students have achieved mastery of the instructional objectives and to assess the effectiveness of instruction. The ABC model evaluation procedures are designed to determine whether a student has achieved mastery of a behavior as specified in the objective assessment items. In the ABC evaluation system, the *Everyone Can* performance objectives, defined as criterion-referenced assessment items, are used for four different purposes: (1) entry and exit assessments; (2) continuous assessment, concurrent with instruction, for the purpose of monitoring the progress of students so that assistance can be given and instruction adjusted; (3) determination of whether components of the instructional model (e.g., instructional blocks, instructional objectives, instructional activities) need modification; and (4) to determine at the end of the instructional block or year whether students and classes have achieved their target expectancies.

STEP ❶
COLLECT
REASSESSMENT DATA

The beauty of the ABC model is that data needed for both student and program evaluation are embedded in the program planning, assessing, implementation planning, and teaching processes. That is, no additional data need be collected to perform the ABC evaluation procedures. For example, all the data needed for student evaluation is contained on the scoresheets for the objectives that have been taught. The key here is that student performance data must be recorded. In chapter 2, on assessment, a case was made for teachers to continually assess and record their students' performance during instruction. We recommended that if teachers could not continually record student assessment (because of class size or limited time) that a strategy be established prior to beginning instruction to periodically record student assessment. Two common data-recording schedules used in physical education are the entry/exit and the entry/middle/exit. Given the scarcity of time for physical education, the entry/ exit option might seem the best choice. But this option has its limitations. If student performance data are collected only at the beginning and end of an instruction block, what happens if you find out at the end of the block that students have made little or no progress? You have used up all your instruction time for this objective before discovering that students are not learning. If you had used the entry/middle/exit schedule, you would have lost only half of your instruction time before your discovery and could have modified your instruction for the second half. Of course if you were continually recording your students' assessment data, you probably would have recognized what was happening after the first week of instruction and had much more time to adjust your instruction. The point is that you need at least entry and exit performance measures on each objective taught in order to do evaluation. The more fre-

quently you record student assessment data, the more efficient you can be in detecting problems and making better use of your instruction time.

In the ABC model, the objective assessment scoresheet is the heart of the evaluation data recording system. At the end of a block of instruction or the end of the year, the scoresheet should contain the record of entry assessment and exit assessment data as well as reflective comments entered by the teacher. These comments summarize any issues or problems encountered while the objective was taught. Figure 5.1 shows a sample objective assessment scoresheet for the catch. Take a moment to review the scoresheet. After the students' names are columns for each of the components of this objective. For the catch there are seven columns: one column for each of the five focal points of skill level 1 and one each for skill levels 2 and 3. There are also three columns to record students' ACE ratings. Remember that these ACE ratings are important for interpreting the validity of the assessment data you have collected. A simple scoring rubric is used to record the assessment results for each student. If on initial (entry) assessment, a student cannot perform the focal point or skill level, an O is put in that cell (e.g., in figure 5.1, Andrew could not perform focal point c). If during initial assessment, a student shows a rudimentary form (i.e., has the idea but still needs more work) of the focal point, then this performance is noted by a slash (/) in the cell (e.g., in figure 5.1, Megan needs more work on focal point c). Finally, if during initial assessment a student demonstrates mastery of the focal point, an X is put in the cell for that focal point (e.g., in figure 5.1, Iva has demonstrated mastery of focal point b). During reassessment, the same symbols are used, only they are recorded over the initial assessment symbols. For example, Liz (in figure 5.1) had an O for stand in the path during initial assessment. At the end of the instruction block, she had mastered this focal point, as indicated by the X over the O. This is just one possible scoring system. Some teachers prefer to write dates in the cells when a focal point is mastered. Others make up their own scoring system. What is important is that you have a method to determine how many focal points of the objective students had at the beginning of the instruction block and how many they have mastered by the end of the block. The sample scoresheet in figure 5.1 also shows the teacher's initial (i.e., cells with dotted background) and target (i.e., cells with lined background) expectations for each student (see chapter 3 for details on setting these expectations). This information is also important for assisting teachers in evaluating the effectiveness of their instruction. Space is also provided on each scoresheet for teachers' reflective comments, which are entered when assessment data are entered. Comments entered during exit assessment are separated by a slash (/). These comments are very helpful for reminding teachers of issues or problems that occurred that might have affected student performance.

STEP ❷
CALCULATE, INTERPRET, AND REPORT STUDENT PERFORMANCE

If you review the completed scoresheet in figure 5.1, you will see that there are six additional columns (A-F) at the right side of the scoresheet. This is where you record evaluation data for use in interpreting student progress. We will now summarize the procedures for calculating the values that go in each of these columns.

1. Student entry score: Identify and enter the number of focal points and skill levels each student has already mastered at the start of the instruction block (i.e., on the initial assessment) and record this value in evaluation column A on the right side of the scoresheet. For example, Megan has an entry score of 2.

2. Student target score: This is the total number of focal points the student is expected to have mastered by the end of the block or year. This number should include both the initial and target expectation focal points, which should be shaded in different colors (shown in figure 5.1 by dotted and lined backgrounds), as well as any focal points already mastered. Record the target number of focal points to be achieved by each student in evaluation column B on the right side of the scoresheet. For example, Aija has a target score of 4.

3. Exit score: Calculate the students' actual exit score for this objective. The exit score is the total number of focal points/skill levels the student has mastered (has earned an X for). For example, Seiji had 3 focal points on the initial assessment at the start of the instruction block. At the end of the block, he had a total of 5 Xs. (Note this is the total number of Xs, including any Xs they had on the initial assessment.) This value is recorded under evaluation column C on the scoresheet.

4. Target met: Determine which students achieved their target expectations set by the teacher by comparing the values in evaluation col-

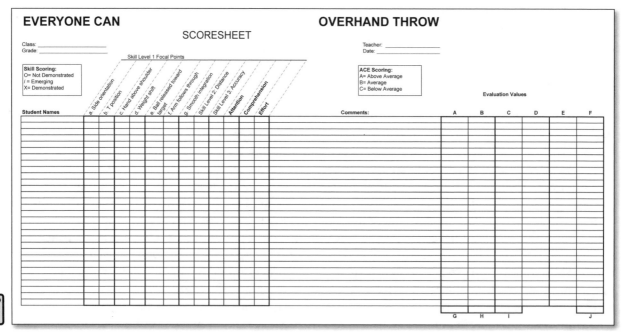

Figure 5.1 Sample scoresheet with pre- and postassessment data and evaluation columns.

umns B and C on the right side of the form. If the exit score (column C) is equal to or greater than the teacher's target expectation (value in column B), then "yes" is recorded in column D. For example, Susan has "yes" in column D because her exit score (2) is equal to her target score (2).

5. Mastery: Determine if the student has mastered the objective. This is determined by comparing the mastery criterion with the exit score. If the exit score equals the mastery criterion, then "yes" is recorded in column E. For example, Jim has "yes" in column E because his exit score is 5, which equals the mastery criterion.

6. Percentage (%) mastery: This value indicates the degree to which the objective has been mastered and is calculated by dividing the student's exit score (evaluation column C) by the mastery criteria (total number of focal points in skill level 1). For example, Andrew has a percentage (%) mastery of 80 because he has mastered 4 of the 5 components of this objective. Note that the mastery criterion for this example was the total number of focal points in skill level 1. Some schools might define their mastery criteria as all the focal points in skill levels 1-3.

With the evaluation data in columns A through F on your objective assessment scoresheets, you now have the information you need to communicate to students and parents how students are performing in physical education. Figure 5.2 shows a simple cumulative progress chart that can be used to communicate to parents and students how the student is doing on the objectives in the program. Although this form does not communicate all the evaluation information available, it does communicate two important things. First, it communicates all the content (i.e., objectives) students are expected to learn in physical education and, specifically, what they are expected to learn each year. Take a moment to review the chart. A row is provided for each grade in the program, and across each row are the 11 objectives targeted to be mastered during that grade. Second, the chart communicates where students started on each objective (E score), how much progress the student has made (X score), and the degree to which the student has mastered each objective (M value). For illustrative purposes, values have been entered for the kindergarten year. Review of these data reveals

that Melissa started this year with mastery of two of the log roll focal points. At the end of the year Melissa had mastered all the focal points of the log roll, which is reflected by an exit score of 8 and 100 percent in the mastery column. Finally, the last column of the report shows the student's overall mastery of all the objectives for that year. This value is calculated by summing the student's percentage of mastery for each objective and then dividing by the number of objectives. For Melissa, this value was 96.36 percent. With this form, a master copy is made for all students and kept in their permanent file. Periodically, the chart is copied and sent home to parents or guardians. Ideally, it should be sent home at the end of each marking period, but at a minimum at the end of each school year.

While the math involved in evaluating student performance, as demonstrated in figure 5.2, is relatively simple, the real challenge is finding the time needed to perform these calculations. For example, a teacher implementing the ABC curriculum presented in this text would teach 10 classes Monday through Friday. Assuming each class has 30 students, this means the teacher has a case load of 300 students. Each student would be working on approximately 11 objectives a year, each of which would have entry, target, and exit scores (300 students × 11 objectives × 3 scores = 9,900). With these 9,900 values (columns A, B, and C on the scoresheets), teachers could then calculate the remaining 9,900 values (columns D-F on the scoresheets) for a total of 19,800 calculations. Finally, this information would then have to be transferred to another document, such as an individual student cumulative progress chart, that could be disseminated to students and parents or guardians.

We do not offer this example to discourage you but to show the amount of time needed to perform student evaluation. Though this process can be done by hand, as illustrated, a far more efficient method is to employ computer technology. Figures 5.3 (p. 88) and 5.4 (p. 90) show parts of a sample computer-generated student progress report. This is typically a one-page report with instructions and objective descriptions reduced to fit on one side and the student progress report on the other. The instructions and objective definitions page is prepared on a word processor. Only one of these pages is required for each grade.

FIGURE 5.2
Sample Individual Student Cumulative Progress Report

Student: Melissa Kelly   **Physical Educator:** Thomas Moran

Class: 2012   **School:** Keswick Elementary

Content	Body parts (5)			Body actions (5)			General space (5)			Follow instructions (5)			Run (5)			Gallop (5)			Even beat (8)			Uneven beat (8)			Log roll (5)			Underhand roll (5)			Underhand throw (5)			Overall Mastery
Grade	E	X	M	E	X	M	E	X	M	E	X	M	E	X	M	E	X	M	E	X	M	E	X	M	E	X	M	E	X	M	E	X	M	
K	2	5	100	3	5	100	1	5	100	2	5	100	1	5	100	0	4	80	2	8	100	1	8	100	2	5	100	2	5	100	2	4	80	96.36

Content	Body planes (3)	Directions in space (4)	Work habits (6)	Hop (4)	Slide (5)	Accented beat (6)	Comm. through move (9)	Shoulder roll (5)	Forward roll (7)	Balance beam walk(2)	Stationary kick (8)
Grade											
1											

Content	Personal space (3)	Skip (5)	Polka (4)	Backward roll (7)	2-point balances (2)	Partial curl-ups (4)	Stretching (4)	Warm-up (4)	CR exertion (3)	Catch (5)	Moving kick (8)
Grade											
2											

Grade 3

Content	Self-respect (4)	Leap (5)	Long jump (5)	Vertical jump (5)	Schottische (4)	1-point balances (2)	Rope jump (5)	Overhand throw (7)	Fielding ground balls (5)	Two-arm sidearm strike (7)	Trap ball (6)

Grade 4

Content	Social skills (6)	Cartwheel (5)	Headstand (6)	Fielding fly balls (8)	Forehand strike (8)	Throw in (6)	Foot dribble (4)	2-hand chest pass (5)	Bounce pass (6)	Forearm pass (6)	Underhand strike (7)

Grade 5

Content	Team play (5)	Endurance run (4)	Push-ups (4)	V-sit reach (5)	BMI (3)	Active lifestyles (3)	Backhand strike (8)	Overhead strike (9)	Hand dribble (5)	Set shot (5)	Overhead pass (6)

Key:

(#) = the number in parentheses after each objective is the number of focal points the student is expected to master.

E = Entry level—the number of focal points the student could perform before instruction.

X = Exit level—the number of focal points the student could perform after instruction.

M = Percentage (%) mastery—the student's exit level divided by the number of focal points in the objective.

Overall mastery = the sum of students' percentage (%) mastery on the 11 objectives taught for that year divided by 11.

FIGURE 5.3

Sample Instructions for Interpreting a Student Evaluation Report

Column heading	Explanation
1. Objectives	The first column of the report contains names or phrases used to label the objectives taught during this reporting period. For more detailed descriptions of the objectives, see the attached objective descriptions or consult the school district physical education curriculum.
2. Entry level	This column contains the student's entry performance level on each objective. Each objective is divided into units called focal points. Entry level indicates the number of focal points the student had achieved prior to instruction. The entry-level score is the basis for measuring improvement.
3. Target exit	This column contains the total number of focal points the teacher expects the student to have achieved on each objective during this reporting period. Target achievement scores are set individually for each student.
4. Actual exit	This column contains the actual number of focal points the student has achieved on each objective at the end of the reporting period.
5. Net change	This column contains the difference between the student's entry and exit performance levels for each objective. This value is indicative of the amount of progress the student made on each objective during this reporting period.
6. Target met	This column contains either a yes or no depending on whether the student's actual exit performance on each objective was equal to or surpassed the target achievement score set by the teacher at the beginning of this instruction period.
7. Mastery criteria	This column contains the mastery criterion for each objective that has been established in the physical education curriculum that all students are expected to achieve. The mastery criterion is the total number of focal points for each objective.
8. Percentage (%) mastery	This column indicates what percentage of the mastery criterion the student has achieved to date on each objective. This value is calculated by dividing the student's actual exit performance score by the mastery criterion for each objective.
9. Class average	This column contains the class average exit performance score for each objective. This value is provided to assist the reader in evaluating a student's performance in relation to the other students in the class. The class average exit value for each objective is the sum of the students' actual exit scores divided by the total number of students in the class for each objective.
10. Teacher comments	This column may contain brief comments or codes provided by the teacher regarding the student's performance on objectives.

ABC School District Physical Education Student Evaluation Report

Description of Physical Education Objectives

The ABC school district physical education curriculum identifies 11 objectives to be mastered during the fourth grade. For more information on these objectives or other objectives in the curriculum, please contact Mr. Kelly.

1. Fielding fly balls is a catching skill used in a variety of ball games and sports such as baseball and is measured by five focal points that define the critical elements that must be performed to successfully field fly balls. The descriptions of these focal points are contained in the physical education curriculum. The desired achievement level (i.e., mastery) is for all students to be able to perform all five focal points for this objective.

2. Forehand strike is a striking skill used in a variety of games and sports such as tennis and is measured by eight focal points that define the critical elements that must be performed to successfully perform a forehand strike. The descriptions of these focal points are contained in the physical education curriculum. The desired achievement level (i.e., mastery) is for all students to be able to perform all eight focal points for this objective.

3. A throw-in is a ball skill used in soccer to put the ball in play from out of bounds and is measured by six focal points that define the critical elements that must be performed to successfully do a throw-in. The descriptions of these focal points are contained in the physical education curriculum. The desired achievement level (i.e., mastery) is for all students to be able to perform all six focal points for this objective.

4. Foot dribble is a ball skill used in a variety of games and sports such as soccer and is measured by four focal points that define the critical elements that must be performed to successfully dribble a ball with the feet. The descriptions of these focal points are contained in the physical education curriculum. The desired achievement level (i.e., mastery) is for all students to be able to perform all four focal points for this objective.

5. Two-hand chest pass is a ball skill used in a variety of games and sports such as basketball and is measured by five focal points that define the critical elements that must be performed to successfully two-hand chest pass a ball. The descriptions of these focal points are contained in the physical education curriculum. The desired achievement level (i.e., mastery) is for all students to be able to perform all five focal points for this objective.

6. Bounce pass is a ball skill used in a variety of games and sports such as basketball and is measured by six focal points that define the critical elements that must be performed to successfully bounce pass a ball. The descriptions of these focal points are contained in the physical education curriculum. The desired achievement level (i.e., mastery) is for all students to be able to perform all six focal points for this objective.

7. Forearm pass is a ball skill used in a variety of games and sports such as volleyball and is measured by six focal points that define the critical elements that must be performed to successfully pass a ball using the forearms. The descriptions of these focal points are contained in the physical education curriculum. The desired achievement level (i.e., mastery) is for all students to be able to perform all six focal points for this objective.

8. Underhand strike is a ball skill used in a variety of games and sports such as volleyball and is measured by seven focal points that define the critical elements that must be performed to successfully strike a ball underhand. The descriptions of these focal points are contained in the physical education curriculum. The desired achievement level (i.e., mastery) is for all students to be able to perform all seven focal points for this objective.

9. Social skills are behaviors needed to participate and play with others in games and sports and are measured by six focal points that define these behaviors. The descriptions of these focal points are contained in the physical education curriculum. The desired achievement level (i.e., mastery) is for all students to be able to perform all six focal points for this objective.

10. Cartwheel is a body-management skill used in a variety of games and sports such as gymnastics and is measured by five focal points that define the critical elements that must be performed to successfully perform a cartwheel. The descriptions of these focal points are contained in the physical education curriculum. The desired achievement level (i.e., mastery) is for all students to be able to perform all five focal points for this objective.

11. Headstand is a body-management skill used in a variety of games and sports such as gymnastics and is measured by six focal points that define the critical elements that must be performed to successfully perform a headstand. The descriptions of these focal points are contained in the physical education curriculum. The desired achievement level (i.e., mastery) is for all students to be able to perform all six focal points for this objective.

Once this page is prepared and saved, it can be reused each year. The individual student progress reports are generated by a computer database management program such as Microsoft Access. A good laser printer could print the 300 student reports needed in our example in less than 10 minutes. Once reports are printed, they are put in the photocopy machine and then instructions and objective definitions are copied on the other side.

Take a moment to review figure 5.4. The objectives taught to this class are listed down the left side of the form in the first column. The entry, target, and exit scores for each objective are shown in the next three columns. Note these are the same values entered by hand in columns A through C on the scoresheet. The next four columns are calculated and filled in by the computer. Net Change is the difference between the

entry and exit values, or the amount of progress made. Target Met corresponds to column D on the scoresheet (figure 5.1, p. 84) and reports yes/no depending on whether the students' exit scores are greater than or equal to their target scores. Mastery Criteria is the number of focal points/skill levels for each objective that must be achieved to master the skill. Percentage (%) Mastery is the degree to which each objective has been mastered. This value is calculated by dividing a student's exit score by the mastery criterion. This value corresponds to column F on the scoresheet (figure 5.1). Class Average shows the average number of focal points/skill levels the class has mastered for each objective. This value is provided so that an individual student's performance can be compared to the class. Finally, the last column is for teacher comments.

FIGURE 5.4
Sample Computer-Generated Progress Report

Student name: Amanda Stewart   Number of students in class: 28   Teacher: Luke Kelly

Grade level: 4th   Report date: May 15, 2007

Objectives	Entry level	Target exit	Actual exit	Net change	Target met	Mastery criteria	% mastery	Class average	Teacher comments
Fielding fly balls	3	5	5	2	Yes	5	100.0	90.4	
Forehand strike	4	7	7	3	Yes	8	87.5	92.7	Excellent progress
Throw-in	4	6	6	2	Yes	6	100.0	98.0	
Foot dribble	3	4	4	1	Yes	4	100.0	96.9	
Two-hand chest pass	2	5	5	3	Yes	5	100.0	99.6	
Bounce pass	3	5	5	2	Yes	6	83.3	97.2	Work on follow-through
Forearm pass	3	6	5	2	No	6	83.3	95.4	More smooth integration
Underhand strike	4	7	7	3	Yes	7	100.0	99.2	
Social skills	4	6	6	2	Yes	6	100.0	98.6	
Cartwheel	2	4	5	3	Yes	5	100.0	96.6	
Headstand	1	4	4	3	Yes	6	66.6	89.6	Needs more practice

Given the professional appearance and ease with which the computer-generated reports can be produced, it would appear that the solution to having teachers do more student evaluation in physical education is simply to give them computers. Although it is true that computer access is virtually essential, this is only part of the solution. The greatest challenge is getting the data into the computer. Some of the necessary data, such as the objective names, student names, and objective mastery criteria, needs to be entered only once. Three of the values (student entry, target, and exit scores), however, must be entered each year for each student on each objective taught in order to produce a report. If you recall from our previous example, this means if you had a case load of 300 students you would still need to enter 9,900 values (300 students × 11 objectives × 3 scores = 9,900) into the computer. These could be entered periodically throughout the year rather than all at one time, but nonetheless they must be entered. The advantage of entering these values into a computer is that the computer can then calculate the remaining 16,500 values (300 students × 11 objectives × 5 values) shown in the student evaluation report in figure 5.4.

Several recent advances in computer technology might provide some assistance in reducing the time spent collecting and entering student performance data into computer databases. Many schools are experimenting with handheld personal digital assistants (PDAs) and the latest notebook computers called PCtablets. These devices are designed to be used by physical educators while they teach. Instead of recording student assessment data on a scoresheet and then later reentering these data into a computer, you directly enter the student assessment data into the PDA/PCtablet, and it is automatically entered into your database. How to use technology in evaluation is discussed later in this chapter (in step 5, p. 96).

Once you have organized your student evaluation data either manually or via computer, you now need to interpret your results and make any necessary adjustments. If students are making acceptable progress, the decision might be to move on to the next objective in the instructional plan. If progress is not acceptable, several questions regarding instruction need to be asked:

1. Were class presentations clear and focused on specific focal points?
2. Did students know specifically what they needed to work on?
3. Did students receive enough explicit feedback during instruction?
4. Was adequate instruction time allotted to the objective?
5. Were students absent a lot?
6. Was time on task lower than 60 percent?
7. Were students developmentally ready to learn the objective?
8. Were success and challenge tasks adequately controlled?
9. What effect could time of day or day of week of instruction have had?
10. Were appropriate instructional activities used? Were they of low interest? Too difficult?
11. Were cues, prompts, and demonstrations appropriate?
12. What effect did class size and size of subgroups have on instruction?
13. Was enough equipment available for each student to be actively involved in activities?
14. Were disruptions during instruction minimal?

If after answering these questions the decision is that instruction was appropriate, but students just did not make enough progress, then the students simply need more instruction time or time on task to master the objective. If the objective is high priority, the decision should be to continue with it and to revise instruction as needed based on the answers to the 14 questions we just looked at. If you find expectations were set too high for students, modify them.

Evaluation of individual student progress might reveal that one or more students is significantly different from the rest of the class with a higher or lower level of performance. Setting realistic target expectancies within the constraints of instruction time and resources takes experience. Teachers should anticipate that initially their expectations for students might be set too high or too low. With experience and time, these estimates will gradually become more reliable and accurate. When a student fails to meet target expectations, consider his or her situation, including absences, sickness, problems that go across classes in school, substitute teachers, and so forth. This is where reflective commentary recorded on the scoresheet can be valuable in reminding teachers of issues and problems that occurred during instruction.

Whatever action is taken, document the adjustment by noting the change on the block teaching learning maps, teacher templates, and student learning formats. This documentation not only improves the quality of instruction but strengthens instructional accountability with parents and administrators. Remember that the ABC program and instructional plan are designed for instructional accountability.

STEP ❸
EVALUATE AND GRADE STUDENTS' PROGRESS

Student evaluation can be either formative or summative. In the ABC model, reassessing a student, identifying an error, and then suggesting an alternative is an example of formative evaluation. Formative evaluation focuses on the process and interprets why certain results occur. Summative evaluation focuses more on overall outcomes of instruction over time. Reporting to a student his or her percentage (%) mastery at the end of an instruction block is an example of summative evaluation. For example, knowing a student is at

80 percent mastery gives you an overall picture of how the student is doing and allows you to compare this performance to another student at, say, 50 percent mastery. Formative and summative evaluation both provide useful information but for different purposes. During learning, students need formative evaluation so they know specifically what errors to correct and how to correct them. However, when you need to report how students are doing overall on the objectives, formative evaluation is too specific and difficult to present and interpret in a meaningful way. A better way to report overall student performance is through summative evaluation in which performance is represented in one value, such as percentage (%) mastery or a letter grade.

Before we discuss how to calculate grades, let's reflect on the purpose of grading. Why do we give grades, and what should the grade represent? In the ABC model, grades are given to focus student attention on what content is to be learned and the degree to which objectives are being mastered. How and what a grade is based on reflects the values of the teacher and the school and communicates to students what is important and where to focus their efforts. Look at the two different grading schemes shown in figure 5.5. What does grading scheme 1 communicate to the student? The first set suggests that what is most important for success in physical education is to show up wearing your gym shoes, smiling, and trying to do what the teacher asks. This will earn you at least a B (i.e., 80 percent). The second grading scheme clearly communicates that what is important is that you master the objectives being taught.

FIGURE 5.5
Comparison of Two Different Grading Schemes

Grading scheme 1		Grading scheme 2	
20%	attendance	0%	attendance
20%	being prepared (gym shoes)	0%	being prepared
20%	attitude/good behavior	0%	attitude/good behavior
20%	effort	0%	effort
20%	objective achievement	100%	objective achievement

The ABC model recommends that grades be based on student achievement of the objectives designated in the program plan and not on prerequisite behaviors for learning such as attitude, effort, or attendance. That is not to say that these prerequisite behaviors are not important. All students need to show up to the learning environment prepared and ready to learn. However, because students are in physical education to learn motor skills, their grade should be based on their achievement of the content.

This sounds simple enough in concept, but how is grading actually done in physical education? What factors should be considered when calculating a grade? Let's assume you have two students working on an objective that has 10 focal points. The first student, Jose, starts the unit with none of the focal points. The teacher sets a target expectation for Jose to learn 3 focal points during the instruction block. At the end of the block, Jose has mastered a total of 4 focal points. Mary, on the other hand, starts the block with mastery of 8 of the 10 focal points. The teacher sets Mary's target expectation at mastering 2 additional focal points. At the end of the block she has mastered 9 of the focal points. How would you grade these two students?

One option is to grade the students based on their overall percentage mastery of the objective. Using this criterion, Jose would be at 40 percent mastery, which would probably translate to an F or U grade. Mary would be at 90 percent mastery, which would probably translate to a grade of A or S. Another option is to grade the students based on their progress or improvement. Using this criterion, Jose would get 100 percent, or an A, because he achieved all three of the target components he was supposed to learn plus an additional component. Mary would get a 50 percent, or an F, because she achieved only one of the two components she was targeted to learn.

What have you learned from this simple example? A grading system based solely on mastery favors the highly skilled students but can be a disincentive for both groups. The highly skilled might be less motivated to work because they already have a passing grade at the start of the instruction block. The low-skilled students might also be unmotivated because they might

perceive that even if they work hard they cannot earn a passing grade. A grading system based on improvement, on the other hand, tends to favor low-skilled students, who have more room to improve, and to disadvantage high-skilled students, who will typically have fewer focal points to learn. An alternative system would be to include and weight grades based on both progress and mastery performance. How heavily each grade would be weighted in the equation would reflect the teacher's values. A simple solution would be to weight both progress and mastery equally at 50 percent. Using the data from our example, Jose would earn an average of 70 percent (40 percent mastery + 100 percent progress / 2 = 70), and Mary would also earn a 70 percent average (90 percent mastery +50 percent progress /2 = 70).

The ABC model does not recommend how progress and mastery should be weighted but does suggest that each school district develop a grading plan consistent with the school's overall grading system. Unfortunately, in many school systems, giving grades in physical education has been dropped or reduced to simple dichotomous systems (e.g., pass/fail or satisfactory/unsatisfactory). This change has occurred largely because physical educators were unable to base their grades on performance data and regressed to using subjective evaluations of effort and attitude as the basis for their grading. Although this may have made grading easier for physical educators, it also undermined the credibility of physical education in the overall school curriculum when it did not use the same grading system as the school's other academic subjects. The issue here is not lack of interest or effort on the part of physical educators but simply time. To compute grades based on weighted percentages of mastery and progress across several objectives for 300+ students every six weeks would require both entry, target, and exit scores as well as the time to perform the necessary calculations. Clearly, this is another situation in which physical educators must harness the power of computer technology. If the student entry, exit, and target scores were already in a database, the software could be programmed to compute weighted grades, which could then be computed and printed in a matter of seconds.

STEP ❹
EVALUATE YOUR PROGRAM

In program evaluation, we are interested in making judgments about the overall impact of the program. Program evaluation is similar to student evaluation only the unit of measure is larger, such as a class or grade level rather than an individual student. Program evaluation examines questions such as these:

- Is the curriculum being implemented as intended?
- How effective was the teaching?
- Are objectives targeted for achievement at the right grade level?

To practically perform program evaluation on a large scale requires the use of computers. However, it is possible to do some basic program evaluation at the class level by hand. Figure 5.6 shows a sample scoresheet used earlier for student evaluation with four additional calculations. To perform these calculations, first compute the four sums indicated by the letters G, H, I, J at the bottom of columns A, B, C, F. Variables G through I contain the sum of the entry, target, and exit scores respectively, and variable J is the sum of the students' percentage (%) mastery. Once you have these values, you can calculate three scores to be used for program evaluation:

- Teacher Effectiveness (TE): This score is calculated by dividing the sum of the class's exit scores (I) by the sum of the class's target scores (H) (39/39 = 1, or 100 percent). The resulting value reflects the degree to which the teacher achieved the expectations set for each student in the class. In this example the teacher's expectations for all students were met, so the teaching effectiveness value was 100 percent.

- Class Mean Gain (CMG): This score is calculated by subtracting the sum of the entry scores (G) from the sum of the exit scores (I) and then dividing the result by the number of students in the class (39 – 17/10 = 2.2). This means that on average students in this class improved 2.2 focal points over the course of this instruction period.

- Class Average Percentage (%) Mastery (CAM): This score is calculated by dividing the sum of the percentage (%) mastery (j) by the number of students in the class (760/10 = 76). This value indicates that at the end of this unit of instruction the class as a whole was at 76 percent mastery for the objective.

Each of these totals provides valuable information, and collectively they provide a good overall

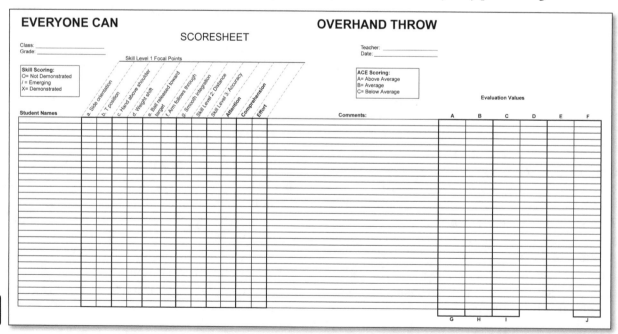

Figure 5.6 Sample scoresheet with program evaluation calculations.

picture of how much learning is occurring. The TE value is an indicator of how well you as the teacher did in achieving the target expectations you set for your students overall. This value is as much a function of the accuracy of a teacher's ability to set realistic expectations as it is of student learning. Ideally, you would like this value in the 85 to 95 percentage range. If this value is consistently below 50 percent, you are probably setting your expectations too high. If it is consistently over 100 percent, you are setting your expectations too low. Obviously, a teacher could easily obtain a high teacher effectiveness rating by simply setting low expectations for students. To control for this, the teacher effectiveness rating should also be interpreted in concert with the class average percentage (%) mastery and class mean gain. If the teacher has a high TE score but low CAM and CMG, then the teacher's effectiveness should be examined.

The CAM provides a summative indicator of how close the class is to achieving an objective. This value must be interpreted in relation to when the objective is targeted to be achieved in the program plan. If the objective is targeted to be achieved this year, this value should be approaching 100 percent.

The CMG informs you of the average number of focal points learned by your students during an instruction period. This value can be used to evaluate if the time allocated in the curriculum is going to be sufficient for this objective to be mastered at the grade level targeted. For example, let's say an objective has 9 focal points and is scheduled to be worked on over three years in the curriculum. If at the end of the first year the CMG is 3, chances are good that this objective can be achieved in the remaining two years.

Although it is probably not practical to do these program evaluation calculations for all your classes by hand, this does not mean no program evaluation should be done. A common adaptation is to randomly pick one class from each grade level and perform the program evaluation calculations on these classes. The results provide valuable insight into both your teaching effectiveness and to the degree the program is being implemented as planned.

Given the magnitude of the data to be manipulated, program evaluation can be greatly enhanced by using a computerized data-management system. Figure 5.7 shows a computer-generated class report that parallels the student report presented earlier. Note that the format of the report is basically the same only the unit of measurement is now a class instead of an individual student. The unit can be any logical grouping, such as a grade level, or a subset, such as females. This report shows in one page how students in a given class performed on all the objectives in the curriculum for one year of the program. The TE values are shown in figure 5.7 under the column heading "% class meeting target." For example, this teacher's effectiveness for the underhand strike was 99.4 percent. The CMG scores are listed in under the column with the same label. For example, the class made an average gain of 3.01 focal points on the forehand strike. Finally, the class's average percentage (%) mastery values are listed under a column with the same label. For example, the data reveals that the class is at 98 percent mastery for the soccer throw-in. In addition, a column has been added in figure 5.7 that shows the percentage (%) of the class that has achieved mastery. This is the number of students who have demonstrated mastery of all the components for the objective divided by the total number of students in the class. For the soccer throw-in that would be 96.55 percent.

Once you have your evaluation data computed, either by hand or via computer, the next step is to interpret your data and take appropriate action. Examine your TE, CAM, and CAG as well as your reflective comments. If progress is not being made as expected, consider some of the following actions. As a rule, start by changing your teaching behavior (e.g., instruction, on-task time, etc.) and then progress to adjusting the program plan as needed.

- Review student evaluation questions (p. 91).
- Revise instruction methods and materials.
- Increase student on-task time.
- Modify expectation levels.
- Add instruction time for the appropriate objective, cutting down on allotted time for another objective or deleting an objective entirely.
- Move this objective to later in the program plan if modifications do not result in adequate student progress.

FIGURE 5.7
Sample Class Report for Program Evaluation

Teacher: Luke Kelly   Number of students in class: 28   Grade level: 4th

Class: Mrs. Moore   Report date: May 15, 2007

Objectives	Class mean entry	Class mean target	Class mean exit	Class mean gain	% class meeting target	Mastery criteria	Class average mastery	% class meeting mastery
Fielding fly balls	2.90	4.80	4.52	1.62	94.16	5	90.4	88.74
Forehand strike	4.41	7.22	7.42	3.01	97.30	8	92.7	90.31
Throw-in	3.22	5.81	5.88	2.59	98.74	6	98.0	96.55
Foot dribble	2.87	3.84	3.88	0.97	99.03	4	96.9	96.75
Two-hand chest pass	2.33	4.92	4.98	2.59	98.79	5	99.6	98.83
Bounce pass	2.75	4.60	4.86	1.85	94.67	6	97.2	95.58
Forearm pass	2.81	5.55	5.72	2.74	96.98	6	95.4	93.91
Underhand strike	3.67	6.90	6.94	3.23	99.40	7	99.2	98.88
Social skills	3.82	5.88	5.92	2.06	99.25	6	98.6	96.76
Cartwheel	2.01	4.58	4.83	2.57	94.79	5	96.6	95.19
Headstand	2.37	5.19	5.38	2.82	96.51	6	89.6	84.29

If expected gains were achieved by students in less than the projected amount of time, note this on the scoresheet and consider the following options for adjustment:

- Set higher levels of expectation and continue instruction on the same objective.
- Discontinue instruction for that objective and move to the next one as scheduled on your program plan.
- Add another objective to the curriculum to fill in the time available.

Although an individual teacher can change his or her behavior (e.g., how an objective is taught), changes to the overall curriculum must be made in concert with all the physical education staff. Changes to the curriculum tend to be based on several data points over time. For example, all teachers working on a given objective are achieving mastery a year before it is scheduled to be achieved in the curriculum. This would be a clear case in which mastery of this objective should be moved to earlier in the curriculum and the time reduced and transferred to other objectives.

Another benefit of program evaluation is that it can be used to identify staff strengths and weaknesses. For example, a program evaluation report can be generated that shows the average percentage (%) mastery by grade, teacher, and objective. Let's say the results show that for a given objective one teacher is obtaining a CAM of 28 percent, whereas another teacher, teaching the same objective to the same grade level, is achieving a CAM of 87 percent. There might be other possible explanations for this difference, but odds are these teachers are teaching this objective different from one another. A common way to handle this situation is to pair the two teachers up so they can observe each other teaching and exchange ideas.

STEP 5
USE TECHNOLOGY TO AID IN EVALUATION

From the discussion of student evaluation, grading, and program evaluation it should be clear that physical educators must harness the power of computer technology if they are going to capitalize on many of the benefits derived from evaluation. Unfortunately, the solution is not as simple as going out and buying a computer program. What is needed to perform student and program evaluation on your computer is a relatively sophisticated database management application that has been specifically designed around your physical education curriculum. Although it is certainly possible that some physical educators could design such a database application using programs such as Access (in the Microsoft Office package), this is not a practical solution for most physical educators. Fortunately, most school systems are currently working on creating system-wide database management programs to manage student performance data in areas such as reading and math. Physical educators need to be proactive and become active participants in this process. Contact your central office and find out who is in charge of this operation for your school district. Often, there will be an advisory committee composed of teachers working on this project. Volunteer to serve on this committee. You need to communicate physical education's data-management needs. Fortunately, if you are using the ABC model, you have all the information you need. You will need to share and explain the following materials to the programmers:

- The program plan—specifically, which objectives are targeted to be achieved at the end of each year of the program
- The scoresheets for each objective in your program plan—specifically, they need to know the number of components for each objective, the mastery criterion, and that three scores (entry, target, exit) will need to be managed on each objective for each student.
- Reports—you need to give them some idea of what type of reports you would like the system to produce and what you would like in each report. You could use the sample reports presented in this chapter as examples and then modify them to meet your needs.

Once the data-management system is in place, the last challenge is developing an efficient method of collecting and entering your student performance data into the system. As discussed earlier in the student evaluation section, many schools are experimenting with using PDAs and tabletPCs as possible solutions to this problem. Although these solutions look promising, it is likely they will not be readily available in many schools or will be too costly in the short term. If so, you need to develop other clever ways to address this problem. Two possibilities are tapping into the talents of your local senior citizens or high school business programs. In many communities, senior citizens love to help the local schools but do not want to work directly with students. These individuals can be excellent volunteers to do data entry. Do not be surprised if you find that many have extensive backgrounds in using computers and can potentially help with other aspects of your physical education data-management system. Many high schools also have business programs designed to prepare high school students for entry-level positions in areas such as data entry. Contact the faculty that runs these programs and investigate ways that your data entry can be used as training opportunities for these students. Remember that whenever you use volunteers you need to regularly thank them for their efforts. Little things like an occasional card, a happy face, or a cup of coffee just to let them know you value them will go a long way toward ensuring a consistent and productive volunteer staff. Also, in your volunteer training you need to include procedures for maintaining confidentiality because volunteers will have access to students' personal data.

STEP ⑥ ESTABLISH PROGRAM ACCOUNTABILITY AND JUSTIFICATION

The importance of accurately reporting student and program effectiveness cannot be overstated. By making significant others aware of your program's effectiveness, you increase the potential for having your program maintained or improved. One of the greatest threats to our physical education programs is ignorance on the part of parents, administrators, and other decision makers. Most adults base their judgments on the purpose and value of physical education on the experiences they had in physical education when they were in school. Unfortunately, few of these adults likely received high-quality objective-based programs as children. The problem is that now, as adults, they do not feel they need to inquire or learn about what is being done in physical education because they think they already know. Our challenge as a profession is to reach out and reeducate the public regarding our programs. One of the ways to do this is through your curriculum and your evaluation procedures. Reexamine the sample student progress report in figures 5.3 (p. 88) & 5.4 (p. 90). If you received this report as a parent, what would it communicate to you about the program? First, you might be surprised how much things have changed. Next, you can see that the report clearly communicates the content your child is being taught, how it is measured, where your child started on the content, what he or she was expected to learn, how much he or she actually did learn, the degree to which each objective has been mastered to date, and how your child is performing in relation to the rest of the students in the class. Some teachers might feel these reports would be overwhelming or too complicated for some parents. That may be the case, especially the first few times you send them home. However, these should be viewed as educational opportunities not as obstacles. What could be a better educational opportunity than a concerned parent calling you and asking for help in understanding their child's progress report? The point here is that we need to reengage parents, administrators, and other decision makers with our physical education programs. Usually the only time most parents and administrators think about physical education is when there is a problem. We need to be proactive and focus their attention on the benefits and outcomes of our programs. Student and program evaluation are excellent ways to start this conversation.

Program and student evaluation are also essential to systematically improving both the curriculum and instruction. Remember that the key elements of the program need to be structured so they can be replicated in other settings and used for staff development if found effective or systematically changed if found ineffective. It is critical that such changes are described and included in the ongoing program. One of the greatest wastes that occurs every year is that hundreds of veteran physical education teachers retire and leave with 30 years of teaching experience in their heads. These veteran teachers are often replaced with new teachers beginning right out of school. These rookies are given a copy of the school's bottom-up curriculum that no one really follows and begin the process of reinventing effective ways to teach their students motor skills. Wouldn't it be far more efficient if new teachers were given a functional curriculum that was actually followed as well as resource materials that other teachers have found effective in teaching this content? The *Everyone Can* resource materials have been created to facilitate this process, but they still need your expertise as a teacher. The *Everyone Can* materials give you a starting place, but when you use them you will adapt and modify them to assist students with different learning needs. When you find a teaching cue that works well or an instructional activity that really helps students with a given focal point, you need to record it to share with other teachers. If you create a great game, instruction activity, target that provides feedback, or any other resource that helps students learn a specific focal point of a skill we encourage you to share it. We have provided forms on the online resource that can be used to record your ideas. We also give information in chapter 8 on how to submit your ideas for consideration to be included in the next edition of *Everyone Can*.

SUMMARY

You should now understand that evaluation in the ABC model is designed to ensure that your physical education program is being implemented as intended and that your students are achieving the objectives targeted to be mastered in your program plan. A strength of the ABC model is that all the data needed for evaluation is built in to the processes of the other components (program planning, assessing, implementation planning, and teaching). To this end, evaluation in the ABC model has two foci: student and program. Student evaluation uses the entry, target, and exit scores recorded on the scoresheets for each objective as the raw data for evaluation. These scores are used to determine whether students have achieved the target expectations set by the teacher and the degree to which they have mastered each objective that has been taught. A subcomponent of student evaluation is grading. Grading is the process of summative evaluation in which student performance across several objectives is represented by a single letter grade or numeric score. Grading is based on the values of both the school and teacher and involves a plan for weighting student progress and mastery so that all students are motivated to achieve in physical education. Program evaluation uses the same three student performance scores used in student evaluation, only the unit of evaluation is larger, such as by class or grade level. Three additional values are calculated to determine the effectiveness of instruction and the degree to which the program is being implemented as intended. These values are teacher effectiveness (TE), class mean gain, (CMG), and class average mastery (CAM). These values along with teacher reflective comments can be used to identify problem areas that are then addressed by identifying the causes and taking appropriate corrective actions. Lack of student gain (i.e., low CMG) might be traced back to finding that several classes during the period while this objective was being worked on were disrupted while a leak in the gym roof was being fixed. Although a leak in the roof is an infrequent occurrence (one would hope), this finding suggests that there is a need for better alternative plans for instruction when the gym is unavailable. Finally, program evaluation can also be used to identify and address staff-development needs. Methods were presented to demonstrate how teachers can perform both student and program evaluation

by hand. However, because of the large student case loads carried by most physical educators, an argument was made for the need for physical educators to harness computer technology to assist them in the evaluation process. In addition to access to a computer, two critical issues must be addressed. First, a database management system must be designed and implemented. This step would typically require the skills of a professional programmer with input from the physical education staff regarding the program objectives, student performance scores, and types of reports desired. Second, a system needs to be created and implemented that facilitates the collecting and entering of student performance data into the computer so that it can be analyzed and meaningful reports generated for student and program evaluation. Finally, a case was made for why it is important for physical educators to proactively use their physical education evaluation data to both justify and communicate the effectiveness of their program to parents, administrators, and other decision makers. Physical educators were also encouraged to modify and expand the *Everyone Can* materials based on their experience and expertise and to record these changes so they could share them with peers and future educators.

We encourage you to complete the chapter's enrichment activities to self-evaluate your understanding of the material presented. Also ask a peer or colleague to evaluate your student and program evaluation knowledge using the evaluation monitoring form at the end of the chapter. The purpose of these activities is to provide you with feedback so you can improve your evaluation methods.

ENRICHMENT ACTIVITIES

These activities should help you understand the major concepts addressed in this chapter. Most teachers find it beneficial to interact with the content. These activities allow you to experiment with the content and see how it works in practice. They can be done individually or in small groups.

1. Get a copy of the grading criteria for physical education for a local school.

What do these criteria communicate to students and parents is most important for getting a good grade in physical education? Interview a few students from this school and find out their interpretation of the grading system and what they think is important for getting a good grade in physical education. Share and discuss your results with peers.

2. Interview a local physical education teacher and ascertain his or her understanding of evaluation and what type of evaluation is done in physical education. Ask questions about what types of data are collected, how they are analyzed, how grades are calculated, and how results are reported to students and parents.

3. Take a scoresheet with entry, target, and exit performance scores for all students and perform the student and program calculations shown in figures 5.2 (p. 86) and 5.7 (p. 96). How long did it take you to do these calculations? What did you learn about your students' individual and class performance when you examined their evaluation data?

4. Identify a parent of an elementary-aged student and share the sample student evaluation report show in figures 5.4 (p. 90) and 5.5 (p. 92). Explain the report to the parent and ask for input. What was their reaction? Ask them what they like about the report. Ask them how this report compares to what they currently receive from their school regarding physical education.

5. Share the sample program evaluation report (figure 5.7, p. 96) with an elementary school administrator. Explain the report and ask for input. Ask what they like about the report. Ask what sort of support would be available to assist physical educators in accessing the computer and technology support in their district.

Evaluation Monitor Form

Teacher's name: _____   Date: _____

Complete the following list of procedures when conducting the final reassessment and evaluation of your program effectiveness. Double-check item 7 when your colleague comes for a visit at the end of the instruction block.

1. Did you have a scoresheet for each objective taught that contains at least entry, target, and exit scores for each student?   ☐ Yes ☐ No

2. Did you determine and record for each student for each objective taught . . .

   a. whether they met your target expectation?   ☐ Yes ☐ No

   b. their percentage (%) mastery?   ☐ Yes ☐ No

   c. whether the objective was mastered?   ☐ Yes ☐ No

3. For students who did not achieve their target expectations, did you . . .

   a. identify why?   ☐ Yes ☐ No

   b. develop a solution to address the problem?   ☐ Yes ☐ No

4. Did you use your student evaluation data to produce meaningful grades for students?   ☐ Yes ☐ No

5. Did you have some form of report to disseminate to students and parents to apprise them of student performance and progress?   ☐ Yes ☐ No

6. For each objective scoresheet, did you compute the program evaluation values:

   a. Sum of class entry scores?   ☐ Yes ☐ No

   b. Sum of class target scores?   ☐ Yes ☐ No

   c. Sum of class exit scores?   ☐ Yes ☐ No

   d. Sum of class percentage (%) mastery?   ☐ Yes ☐ No

   e. Teacher effectiveness (TE)?

   f. Class average percentage (%) mastery (CAM)?   ☐ Yes ☐ No

   g. Class mean gain (CMG)?   ☐ Yes ☐ No

7. If your TE, CAM, CMG values were less than satisfactory, did you . . .

   a. identify possible causes for these deficits?   ☐ Yes ☐ No

   b. develop solutions to address these problems?   ☐ Yes ☐ No

8. Did you have some form of report to summarize the effectiveness of your teaching and your program?   ☐ Yes ☐ No

9. Did you disseminate your program evaluation report to . . .

   a. your principal?   ☐ Yes ☐ No

   b. your director of physical education?   ☐ Yes ☐ No

10. Did you record any changes to your . . .

   a. Program plan?   ☐ Yes ☐ No

   b. Block teaching learning maps?   ☐ Yes ☐ No

   c. Teaching templates?   ☐ Yes ☐ No

   d. Student learning formats?

   e. *Everyone Can* objective assessment items?   ☐ Yes ☐ No

   f. *Everyone Can* instruction activities?   ☐ Yes ☐ No

   g. *Everyone Can* games?   ☐ Yes ☐ No

   h. *Everyone Can* station task cards?   ☐ Yes ☐ No

PART II

EVERYONE CAN!

ONLINE RESOURCES

MODEL K-5 PHYSICAL EDUCATION PROGRAM PLAN

What we will describe in this chapter is a model program plan developed by the elementary physical education teachers in the Highland School District. We want to stress at the outset that this is a model curriculum designed around the unique conditions of one hypothetical school district. Because every school district is unique in terms of teacher talent, instruction time available, student abilities, and resources allocated to support physical education, this curriculum is not designed to be adopted by other schools without considering those factors.

To develop a functional physical education curriculum that will work in your school district, you and your colleagues should go through the ABC planning process and develop a curriculum around your local attributes and constraints. This model curriculum is designed to highlight what can be accomplished in physical education under rather idealistic conditions. For example, the elementary schools in the Highland School District have physical education instruction five times a week with 30 minutes for each class. The programs are all delivered by experienced physical education specialists, and the average class size is 25 students. The school district is well supported by the local community, and as a result the physical education program is valued and provided with adequate facilities and equipment. The result of these advantageous conditions is that the curriculum developed in this chapter can include more content than most elementary programs can address. The advantage here is that we have developed and supplied instruction materials for

all these objectives in the *Everyone Can* resource materials. Because most schools will only be able to address a subset of the objectives provided in the model curriculum, we hope we have provided instruction materials for all the objectives you require for your curriculum.

Our purpose in this chapter is to illustrate the five steps in the ABC planning process along with the worksheets and products produced at the end of each of these steps. The five ABC planning steps covered in this chapter are summarized in table 6.1 and are keyed to the steps and to pages in chapter 1 where they are addressed and to the products that are produced.

Model K-5 Physical Education Program Plan Steps

1. Develop program philosophy, goals, and objectives.
2. Establish program goal emphasis.
3. Calculate instruction time and average mastery time.
4. Calculate amount of content to include in the curriculum.
5. Sequence content across the curriculum.
6. Create yearly and block teaching and learning maps.

Table 6.1 ABC Planning Steps, Processes, and Products

Steps	Chapter 1 Page #	Key processes	Products
1	5	Define the curriculum philosophy, goals, and objectives: form the curriculum development team, establish a common philosophy, create curriculum goals, and list and rank order possible objectives under each goal.	A written philosophy statement, a list of program goals, and a rank-ordered list of objectives for each goal that indicate what students will achieve by the end of the program.
2	11	Establish the program goal. Emphasis: determine the emphasis each goal should receive across grades K-5.	A table that illustrates the percentage of emphasis of time devoted to each curriculum goal by grade and across the curriculum.
3	12	Calculate available instruction time and average objective mastery time.	A table that illustrates the actual amount of instruction time available for the program. A table that produces a single time estimate that represents the amount of time needed to teach and achieve mastery of an average objective in the curriculum.
4	14	Calculate the total number of objectives that can be included in the curriculum.	A table that illustrates the calculations and the number of objectives that will be included in the curriculum for each curriculum goal.
5	15	Sequencing the objectives across the curriculum: using the ranked lists of objectives for each goal to determine the specific objectives that will be included; using developmental principles and the implementing-up concept; determining when instruction will be initiated and when mastery is expected.	A program plan that indicates at what grade level instruction will begin on each objective and when each objective will be mastered so the stated curriculum goals are achieved by all students by the end of the program.
6	18	Create yearly and block teaching learning maps that indicate how the objectives targeted for instruction for each year of the program will be grouped for instruction.	A yearly teaching learning map for each year of the program and a block teaching learning map for each block in each yearly teaching learning map.

STEP 1
DEVELOP PROGRAM PHILOSOPHY, GOALS, AND OBJECTIVES

The program planning process begins by creating a program philosophy, program goals, and rank-ordered lists of objectives for each goal. The program philosophy addresses these questions: Why do students need this program? How will they benefit from it? The philosophy for the program is informed by the values and beliefs of the physical educators, staff, students, school administration, and community. Program goals define what students will be able to do when they complete the program; program objectives define what content students must master to achieve the goals.

Program Philosophy and Goals

The Highland School District includes five elementary schools, two middle schools, and one high school. The school district is going through a curriculum review and revision process and has decided to revise its elementary curriculum this year with revisions to the middle school and high school curricula to follow in subsequent years. A curriculum committee comprised of the five elementary physical education teachers, two community representatives, an elementary school principal, and an assistant superintendent from the central office was created. The first tasks for this committee are to discuss the role and value of physical education in Highland and to develop a philosophy statement for their program. The committee starts by reviewing literature related to the roles, purposes, and benefits of physical education. The committee also reviews national standards (e.g., NASPE standards) and their state physical education standards. These materials are then discussed and included in a program philosophy statement. At the end of the philosophy statement, the committee lists goals that describe what students will achieve by the end of the program. The Highland elementary physical education philosophy statement is shown on page 7.

Program Objectives

Although the program goals provide general description of what students will be able to do at the end of the program, they remain rather broad statements of educational intent. For example, the last goal proposed by the Highland teachers is that students will leave the program with the fundamental object control skills they need to learn and participate in a variety of societal games and sports. What specific motor skills are these? If two teachers were to make a list of these skills, would they list the same skills? This is where the design down or top-down part of the ABC planning is executed. Each goal is task analyzed to identify all the skills or objectives needed to achieve the goal. After lists of objectives are created for each goal area, teachers rank the objectives from most to least important in terms of their contribution to the goal. A process called the consensus forming technique is then used to produce an overall ranking for the objectives within each goal. The consensus forming technique is described in figure 6.1.

FIGURE 6.1
Consensus-Forming Technique

1. List the competing items or issues and assign each a unique number from 1 to x (where x is the number of the last item in the list).

2. Have each member independently rate, or rank, the items from highest priority (1) to lowest priority (x). All items must be ranked, and all items must be assigned a unique rank—no ties.

3. Collect the individual rankings, compute the average ranks for each item, and then relist the items in rank order from 1 to x based on the calculated average ranks.

4. Provide members a timed individual opportunity to address why they believe any item should either be moved farther up or down the list. All comments must be directed to the content in question; no personal references to the comments of other members should be allowed. Depending on the complexity of the issue, a time limit should be placed on the individual comments ranging from 1 to 3 minutes. Each member should systematically be provided with an opportunity to speak to the rankings. This process is designed to rein in the domineering, overly verbal members and to encourage the quiet, less verbal members to participate.

5. After the comment period, all members again rank the items. This process allows individuals to reflect on the insights, new information, and comments that have been made and to indicate the impact on their rankings of the items.

6. Compute average ranks for each item and relist the items in rank order from 1 to x based on the calculated average ranks.

7. Repeat steps 4 through 6 until the relative rankings stabilize. Although the actual average ranks (values) will vary after each re-ranking, as soon as the items stay in the same order for two consecutive rankings, consensus has been reached. Once consensus is reached, the issue is closed to further discussion during the planning process.

Reprinted, by permission, from L.E. Kelly and V.J. Melograno, 2004, *Developing the physical education curriculum: An achievement-based approach* (Champaign, IL: Human Kinetics), 107.

Table 6.2 shows the results of the Highland teachers' rankings after using the consensus forming technique for the first program goal area of body awareness. To start, the teachers made a comprehensive list of all the objectives they thought students should learn under this goal area. This content in the form of objectives is listed down the left side of table 6.2. Next, each teacher individually ranked the importance of these objectives. Teachers were asked: "If you could teach only one objective under this goal, which objective would you teach?" This objective is given the rank of 1. The process is repeated, assigning subsequent numbers to each objective until all objectives are ranked. Table 6.2 shows the rankings for the five Highland physical education teachers at the end of the third round of the consensus forming technique. The values in the last column on the right are the averages of the five teachers' rankings for each

objective. The number in parentheses represents the absolute rank for the objectives based on the averages. For example, the average ranking for the body parts objective is 1.4. Because this is the lowest average rank for all the objectives, this objective receives the absolute rank of 1. Balance, on the other hand, has an average rank of 8.0. Because this is the largest average rank among the objectives, this objective receives an absolute rank of 9. According to the consensus forming technique, when the absolute ranks do not change between two consecutive rounds, you have reached consensus. The consensus forming technique was performed by the Highland physical educators on all the objectives for the remaining goal areas. The results of these ranks are shown in table 6.3. The values in table 6.3 represent the final absolute rankings. To make the charts easier to read, objectives have been relisted in rank order.

Table 6.2 Process for Rank-Ordering Objectives Within Goal Areas

Consensus Forming Worksheet

Goal Area: Body Awareness Ranking Round: 3

Objectives	Teacher 1	Teacher 2	Teacher 3	Teacher 4	Teacher 5	Final
Body parts	1	3	1	1	1	1.4 (1)
Personal space	3	1	2	4	4	2.8 (2)
Directionality	8	9	3	6	9	7.0 (7)
Body actions	2	4	4	5	2	3.4 (3)
Directions in space	5	5	6	7	6	5.8 (6)
Spatial awareness	7	8	7	9	8	7.8 (8)
Body planes	6	6	8	2	5	5.4 (5)
General space	4	2	5	3	3	3.8 (4)
Balance	9	7	9	8	7	8.0 (9)

Table 6.3 Final Objective Rank Orders for the Seven Program Goals

Goal area	Objectives	Final rank
Body awareness	Body parts	1
	Personal space	2
	Body actions	3
	General space	4
	Body planes	5

Goal area	Objectives	Final rank
	Directions in space	6
	Directionality	7
	Spatial awareness	8
	Balance	9
Personal/social	Follows instructions	1
	Work habits	2
	Self-respect	3
	Social skills	4
	Team play	5
	Self-advocacy	6
	Respect for equipment	7
	Cooperation	8
	Sportsmanship	9
Locomotor skills	Run	1
	Gallop	2
	Hop	3
	Slide	4
	Skip	5
	Leap	6
	Long jump	7
	Vertical jump	8
	Run backward	9
	Combination skills	10
Rhythm and dance	Even beat	1
	Uneven beat	2
	Accented beat	3
	Communication through movement	4
	Polka	5
	Schottische	6
	Square dance	7
	Line dance	8
	Creative dance	9
Body control	Log roll	1
	Shoulder roll	2

(continued)

Table 6.3 *(continued)*

Goal area	Objectives	Final rank
	Forward roll	3
	Backward roll	4
	Two-point balances	5
	One-point balances	6
	Rope jump	7
	Balance beam walk	8
	Cartwheel	9
	Headstand	10
	Handstand	11
	Kip-up	12
	Round-off	13
Physical fitness	Partial curl-ups	1
	Endurance run	2
	Push-ups	3
	V-sit reach	4
	Body mass index	5
	Stretching	6
	Warm-up	7
	Active lifestyle	8
	Cardiorespiratory exertion	9
	Speed	10
	Power	11
	Skinfolds	12
Object control skills	Underhand roll	1
	Underhand throw	2
	Overhand throw	3
	Catch	4
	Fielding fly balls	5
	Fielding ground balls	6
	Two-arm sidearm strike	7
	Forehand strike	8
	Backhand strike	9
	Overhand strike	10
	Kick stationary ball	11

Goal area	Objectives	Final rank
	Kick moving ball	12
	Trap ball	13
	Throw-in	14
	Foot dribble	15
	Two-hand chest pass	16
	Bounce pass	17
	Hand dribble	18
	Set shot	19
	Forearm pass	20
	Overhand pass	21
	Underhand strike	22
	Frisbee throw	23
	Lay-up	24
	Punting	25
	Jump shot	26
	Rebounding	27
	Tennis volley	28

STEP ❷
ESTABLISH PROGRAM GOAL EMPHASIS

One of the unique features of the ABC planning process is that it considers factors such as available instruction time, teacher competency, and class size when determining how much content should be included in the curriculum. Failure to consider such factors can frequently result in teachers trying to teach too much content in too little time. This can result in students not mastering the content and subsequently not achieving the goals of the curriculum. The first step in determining how much content can be included in your curriculum is to establish the program goal emphasis for the curriculum. The program goal emphasis in turn will determine how much content can be included in the curriculum for each goal. To perform this step, the Highland physical education teachers created a chart with goals listed down the left side and the grades in the program listed across the top (table 6.4). Each teacher independently completes the chart, indicating how much emphasis should be given to each goal at each grade. It is imperative that only 100 percent is allocated in each column/grade across the goals. As we mentioned in chapter 1, a simple spreadsheet can be created in Excel to simplify summing the numbers and deriving the correct totals for each column. To achieve consensus, individual teacher values are averaged, and the consensus forming technique is used. The data shown in table 6.4 are the final results of the consensus forming process. Each value in the table represents the average of the emphasis assigned to each goal area by summing the individual teacher values and then dividing by five. To compute the final program emphasis for each goal, the values across each row are summed and then divided by the number of grades (i.e., 6). For example, the sum of the emphasis values for health and fitness is 84. This value is divided by 6, the number of grade levels in the program,

Table 6.4   Final Program Goal Emphasis Worksheet

Goal area	K	1	2	3	4	5	Program emphasis
Body awareness	27	18	9				9.0%
Personal/social	10	10	7	7	7	7	8.0%
Locomotor	18	18	9	9	9	9	12.0%
Rhythm and dance	18	18	9	9			9.0%
Body control	9	27	18	18	18		15.0%
Health and fitness			12	21	21	30	14.0%
Object control	18	9	36	36	45	54	33.0%
Sum = 100%	100	100	100	100	100	100	100%

* Each value in the chart represents the teachers' average percent ratings.

and the program weight is 14 percent. This means that the Highland teachers want to spend approximately 14 percent of their instruction time in their physical education program on physical fitness.

STEP ❸
CALCULATE INSTRUCTION TIME AND AVERAGE MASTERY TIME

To determine how much content can be taught and mastered by students in the program you need to do two time calculations. First, determine how much instruction time is available for the program across all grades included in the program. Then calculate the average amount of time students need to master a typical objective in the program.

Instruction Time

Now the Highland physical education teachers need to determine how much time they have available for their physical education program. To calculate this, they review the instruction time worksheet shown in table 6.5. This chart shows how much time is available for physical education based on the number of days of physical education instruction provided each week. The chart is based on physical education being taught for 30 minutes each class period and the school year being 36 weeks in length. If these values are

different for your school district, you will need to revise the worksheet before calculating your time. After the total time is calculated in column 5, 10 percent of this time is removed to cover lost instruction time caused by uncontrollable circumstances such as the use of the gym for assemblies, teacher sick days, and school closings for bad weather. Because the Highland School District has physical education five times a week, they have a total of 29,160 minutes (486 hours) for physical education across the six years of their program. The last column of table 6.5 shows the amount of time available for physical education in hours for each year in the program. Some teachers are surprised to learn how little time they have for physical education. For example, if you have physical education only twice a week, you have only 32.4 hours of instruction time with each of your classes across an entire year.

Average Objective Mastery Time

The Highland physical educators now need to figure out how long it takes them to teach an average objective in their curriculum. To calculate this, they need to estimate how long it takes them individually to teach a typical class mastery of common physical education objectives. This process further adjusts the curriculum to meet the unique needs of the district. For example, if a school district has large class sizes, or if they combine two classes for physical education, they would require more time to teach an objective than another school district that had small class sizes. So how is average objective mastery time calculated? Ideally, teachers estimate how long it takes them to teach each objective in the program and then complete a consensus form on these values. Unfortunately, this is very time consuming and tedious for teachers to do. It is also redundant because many objectives require similar amounts of time. To facilitate the process, then, teachers are asked to select a sample objective from the list of rank-ordered objectives identified for each goal area (see table 6.3, p. 108). This sample objective should be representative of how long it typically takes to teach an objective in this goal area. Table 6.6 shows down the left side the sample objectives the Highland teachers selected for each of their program goals. Note it is

important at this time for the teachers to discuss what is meant by mastery so they are all rating the same thing. Using the *Everyone Can* materials, this is a relatively straightforward process. Once a sample objective is identified for each goal area, the objective assessment items for these objectives are reviewed. Figure 6.2 shows an example of an *Everyone Can* objective assessment item for the overhand throw. The Highland teachers reviewed the *Everyone Can* objective assessment items for their seven sample objectives and decided to define mastery for their curriculum as all students demonstrating skill level 1. Each Highland teacher then reviews the skill level 1 focal points for each of the sample objectives and makes an independent estimate of how long it would take them to teach a typical class mastery of the objective identified for each goal area. Table 6.6

Table 6.5   Instruction Time Worksheet

Number of classes per week	Number of weeks per year	Number of minutes per class	Number of grades	Total minutes	Minus 10%	Minutes available	Minutes per year	Hours per year
1	36	30	6	6,480	-648	5,832	972	16.2
2	36	30	6	12,960	-1,296	11,664	1,944	32.4
3	36	30	6	19,440	-1,944	17,496	2,916	48.6
4	36	30	6	25,920	-2,592	23,328	3,888	64.8
5	36	30	6	32,400	-3,240	29,160	4,860	81.0

Table 6.6   Estimating Mastery Times Goal Areas Using Representative Objectives

Program goal	Sample objective	Teacher ratings					
		1	2	3	4	5	Avg.
Body awareness	Body actions	120	400	300	360	420	320
Personal/social	Follows instructions	180	360	400	320	340	320
Locomotor	Skip	360	420	440	480	600	460
Rhythm and dance	Polka	360	380	340	400	420	380
Body control	Backward roll	360	460	440	360	380	400
Health and fitness	Partial curl-ups	500	600	640	420	440	520
Object control	Overhand throw	420	600	560	400	520	500

shows the final summary of the Highland teachers' estimates, with the last column showing the average estimate (i.e., the sum of the teachers' independent estimates divided by the number of teachers) for each of the sample objectives.

Now that the Highland physical educators know how long it will take to teach a typical objective in each of the goal areas, they need to weight these estimates according to the program goal. To do this they multiply the average mastery time estimate for each sample objective calculated in table 6.6 times the program goal emphasis values calculated earlier in table 6.4. What this

does is weight the time estimate by the amount of time that should be spent on the objectives in each goal area across the entire curriculum. The overall average objective mastery time based on the Highland teachers' estimates is 441.6 minutes. This value is calculated by summing the estimated time by goal weights for each of the program goal areas, as shown in column C in table 6.7. This value indicates that the Highland physical educators estimate that it will require, on average, 441 minutes to teach a class of 25 students mastery of the skill level 1 focal points for a typical objective in their curriculum.

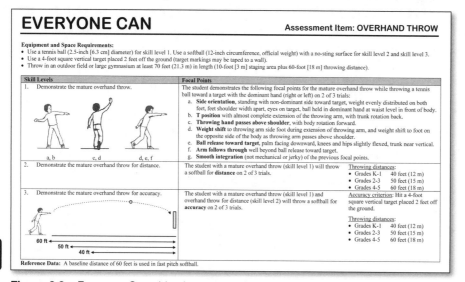

Figure 6.2 *Everyone Can* objective assessment item for the overhand throw.

Illustrations reprinted from J. Wessel, 1976, *I can: Object control* (North Brook, IL: Hubbard Scientific Company), 35. By permission of J. Wessel.

Table 6.7 Calculating the Average Objective Mastery Time for the Curriculum

Category	(a) Estimated average (from table 6.6)	(b) Program % goal emphasis (from table 6.4)	(c) Estimated time by goal weight (a) X (b)
Body awareness	320	9%	28.8
Personal/social	320	8%	25.6
Locomotor	460	12%	55.2
Rhythm and dance	380	9%	34.2
Body control	400	15%	60.0
Health and fitness	520	14%	72.8
Object control	500	33%	165.0
Sum	2,900	100%	441.6

STEP ❹
CALCULATE AMOUNT OF CONTENT TO INCLUDE IN THE CURRICULUM

Now that the Highland physical education teachers know how much time is available in their program and how long it takes to teach a typical objective, they can calculate how much content can be included in their curriculum. In table 6.5 the Highland teachers calculated that they had a total of 29,160 minutes of physical education time available across grades K through 5. From table 6.6, the teachers learned that it takes 441.6 minutes on average to achieve mastery of a typical objective in their curriculum. Dividing the time available (29,160 minutes) by the time needed to teach mastery of an average objective (441.6 minutes) results in a total of 66 objectives that can be taught in the Highland elementary curriculum.

The Highland physical educators now know exactly how many objectives to include in their curriculum, so it is time to determine how many of these objectives to include in each of their seven goal areas. To make this calculation, they simply multiply the program goal emphasis for each goal area (shown in table 6.4) times the total number of objectives that can be included in the curriculum (66), as shown in table 6.8.

Now that they know how many objectives can be included in their curriculum in each goal area, the Highland teachers need only go back to the rank-ordered lists of objectives for each goal reported in table 6.3 and select the appropriate number of objectives according to their rank. For example, according to table 6.8, a total of six body awareness objectives can be included in the curriculum. To determine which six objectives should be included, the teachers return to table 6.3 and under body awareness select the objectives ranked 1 through 6 (body parts, personal space, body actions, general space, body planes, and directions and space). The last three objectives will not be included because there is insufficient time in the curriculum. This process is repeated for the remaining six goal areas. Figure 6.3 shows the final 66 objectives that will be included in the Highland elementary curriculum based on their rank order within the goal areas.

STEP ❺
SEQUENCE CONTENT ACROSS THE CURRICULUM

The Highland teachers now know what content to include in their curriculum. The next step is to sequence the identified objectives across the grades in the program developmentally so that they will be taught at the appropriate time. Although development frequently influences how objectives were initially ranked in step 1, the objectives were actually ranked in terms of their

Table 6.8 Calculating the Number of Objectives for Each Program Goal

Goal area	Program goal emphasis	Total number of program objectives	Number of objectives for this goal
Body awareness	9.0%	66	6
Personal/social	8.0%	66	5
Locomotor	12.0%	66	8
Rhythm and dance	9.0%	66	6
Body control	15.0%	66	10
Health and fitness	14.0%	66	9
Object control	33.0%	66	22
Total =	100%	66	66

FIGURE 6.3
Top Ranked Objectives by Goal Area

Body Awareness

Body parts
Body actions
Body planes
General space
Directions in space
Personal space

Personal/Social

Follows instructions
Work habits
Self-respect
Social skills
Team play

Body Control

Log roll
Shoulder roll
Forward roll
Backward roll
Two-point balances
One-point balances
Rope jump
Balance beam walk
Cartwheel
Headstand

Locomotor

Run
Gallop
Hop
Slide
Skip
Leap
Long jump
Vertical jump

Rhythm and Dance

Even beat
Uneven beat
Accented beat
Communication
Polka
Schottische

Health and Fitness

Partial curl-ups
Endurance run
Push-ups
V-sit reach
BMI
Stretching
Warm-up
Active lifestyle
Cardiorespiratory exertion

Object Control

Underhand roll
Underhand throw
Overhand throw
Catch
Fielding fly balls
Fielding ground balls
2-arm sidearm strike
Forehand strike
Backhand strike
Overhand strike
Kick stationary ball
Kick moving ball
Trap ball
Throw-in
Foot dribble
Two-hand chest pass
Bounce pass
Hand dribble
Set shot
Forearm pass
Overhand pass
Underhand strike

importance. Thus, the teachers need to reexamine the objectives in terms of when they are achieved by students developmentally and then sequence them across the grades in the program.

Using the objective lists shown in figure 6.3, the Highland teachers now distribute the objectives across the six years in their program. Using the program goal emphasis worksheet created in step 2 as a guide, they distribute the objectives across the program. The goals/objectives should be listed down the left side of the table and the grades across the top (table 6.9). For each objective, three codes are entered into the table: when instruction should start (- -), when the objective is expected to be mastered (**), and, if appropriate, when time will be allocated for review (R). Remember that during this phase the average

objective mastery time for each objective can and should be distributed across multiple years in the program for most objectives so they are mastered in the year indicated. The other rule for this table is that a certain number of objectives should be targeted for mastery during each year. For the Highland Elementary curriculum they have 81 hours of instruction time each year, and they estimated that it would require approximately 441 minutes to master an average objective. Using these values, they should target 11 objectives for mastery each year (81 hours converted to minutes = 4,860 divided by 441.6 = 11). Rather than using the consensus forming technique, the Highland school teachers just made a table on a blackboard and discussed where each objective should be placed. The final results are shown in table 6.9.

Table 6.9 Sequencing Program Objectives Developmentally Across the Grades in the Program

Goal area	Objective	Grades					
		K	1	2	3	4	5
Body awareness	Body parts	**					
	Body actions	**					
	Body planes	--	**				
	General space	**					
	Directions in space	--	**				
	Personal space		--	**			
Personal/social	Follows instructions	**	R				
	Work habits	--	**	R			
	Self-respect		--	--	**	R	
	Social skills			--	--	**	R
	Team play					--	**
Locomotor	Run	**					
	Gallop	**					
	Hop	--	**				
	Slide	--	**				
	Skip		--	**			
	Leap			--	**		
	Long jump			--	**		
	Vertical jump			--	**		
Rhythm and dance	Even beat	**					
	Uneven beat	**					
	Accented beat	--	**				
	Communication through movement	--	**				
	Polka			**			
	Schottische				**		
Body control	Log roll	**					
	Shoulder roll	--	**				
	Forward roll	--	**				
	Backward roll		--	**			
	Two-point balances		--	**			

(continued)

Table 6.9   *(continued)*

Goal area	Objective	Grades					
		K	1	2	3	4	5
	One-point balances			--	**		
	Rope jump		--	--	**		
	Balance beam walk		**				
	Cartwheel				--	**	
	Headstand				--	**	
Physical fitness	Partial curl-ups			**			
	Endurance run		--	--	--	--	**
	Push-ups				--	--	**
	V-sit reach					--	**
	Body mass index						**
	Stretching	--	--	**	R	R	
	Warm-up	--	--	**	R	R	
	Active lifestyle					--	**
	Cardiorespiratory exertion	--	--	**	R	R	
Object control	Underhand roll	**					
	Underhand throw	**					
	Overhand throw		--	--	**		
	Catch	--	--	**			
	Fielding fly balls				--	**	
	Fielding ground balls			--	**		
	Two-arm sidearm strike		--	--	**		
	Forehand strike				--	**	
	Backhand strike					--	**
	Overhand strike					--	**
	Kick stationary ball	--	**				
	Kick moving ball	--	--	**			
	Trap ball		--	--	**		
	Throw-in				--	**	
	Foot dribble			--	--	**	
	Two-hand chest pass			--	--	**	
	Bounce pass			--	--	**	
	Hand dribble				--	--	**

118

Goal area	Objective	Grades					
		K	1	2	3	4	5
	Set shot				--	--	**
	Forearm pass			--	--	**	
	Overhand pass				--	--	**
	Underhand strike			--	--	**	

** = mastery expected by the end of this grade.
- - = objective is introduced or worked on during this grade.
R = objective is reviewed or time is allocated for maintenance.

STEP ❻
CREATE YEARLY AND BLOCK TEACHING AND LEARNING MAPS

Now that the scope and the sequence of the curriculum have been determined, the Highland physical education teachers can develop their yearly and block teaching and learning maps, as discussed in chapter 1. This step can be done individually, but we recommend that the initial maps be developed by groups of teachers. Once teachers have implemented the maps for a few years, they will gradually individualize them. Table 6.10 shows a YTLM for the fourth grade of the Highland physical education curriculum. To create this table, the teachers needed to review and identify the content that had to be taught during this year. Reviewing figure 6.3, they determined that 11 objectives were targeted for mastery, 4 objectives required continued review, and 10 objectives were slated for either continued or initial instruction during this year. After analyzing and discussing the various objectives, the teachers decided to divide the fourth year into nine four-week blocks and group the objectives into four blocks that would be repeated twice and a concluding block with an emphasis on fitness before the students left for the summer. Using a spreadsheet, the teachers then systematically sequenced the content across the year according to the objective groupings they created. To keep table 6.10 easier to read, the actual minutes assigned to each objective have been omitted, but they would normally be included and managed in this spreadsheet. Two codes are used in the chart to distinguish objectives being reviewed from objectives that are the primary foci of instruction. For example, the students have already mastered the self-respect, warm-up, and stretching objectives. However, these objectives are integrated into all the current blocks and are reviewed as needed during the year. Other objectives, such as the fitness objectives, are introduced in lessons systematically across the blocks and then incorporated into the warm-up routine done at the start of each lesson. Finally, the remaining objectives are targeted for concentrated blocks of instruction across the various blocks created for this year.

As you recall from chapter 1, the YTLMs provide the foundation for creating block teaching learning maps (BTLMs). The BTLMs delineate how objectives identified in each block in the YTLM will be distributed across the instruction days in the block. Table 6.11 shows a sample BTLM for the first ball skills block for the fourth grade. The objectives to be addressed in this block, taken from table 6.10, are listed down the left side of the block, and the instruction days in the block are listed across the top of the chart. Codes are entered into the chart to indicate when each objective will be addressed and how (e.g., A = initial assessment, F = formal instruction, etc.)

The codes in the BTLM also provide an outline that can be translated into a teaching template or lesson plan. For example, let's look at Wednesday of the second week of the BTLM in table 6.11 and see how one of the Highland teachers has turned this information into a teaching plan shown in table 6.12. The chart indicates

Table 6.10 Sample Yearly Teaching Learning Map for the Fourth Grade

Instruction Blocks - 9 × 4 weeks

Objectives	Status	Ball skills	Striking	X-games	Ball skills	Striking	X-games	Ball skills	Striking	Fitness
Social skills	M		X	O	O	O	O	O	O	O
Team play	I							X	O	O
Self-respect	R	X	O	O	O	O	O	O	O	O
Cartwheel	M			X			X			
Headstand	M			X			X			
Endurance run	I		X	O	O	O	O	O	O	O
Cartwheel	M			X			X			
Push-ups	I			X	O	O	O	O	O	O
V-sit	I			X	O	O	O	O	O	O
Active lifestyle	I		X							X
Stretching	R	X	O	O	O	O	O	O	O	O
Warm-up	R	X	O	O	O	O	O	O	O	O
CR Exertion	R		X	O	O	O	O	O	O	X
Fielding fly balls	M	X			X			X		X
Foot dribble	M	X			X			X		X
Throw-in	M	X			X			X		X
Hand dribble	I	X			X			X		
Two-hand chest pass	M	X			X			X		X
Bounce pass	M	X			X			X		X
Set shot	I				X			X		
Forehand strike	M		X			X			X	X
Backhand strike	I		X			X			X	
Overhand strike	I		X			X			X	
Forearm pass	M		X			X			X	X
Underhand strike	M		X			X			X	X
Overhead pass	I		X			X			X	

Status codes
M = to be mastered this year
I = continued instruction during this year
R = already mastered but reviewed this year

Matrix codes
X = focus of instruction during this unit
O = ongoing practice/review during this unit

that three objectives (self-respect, stretching, and warm-up) require ongoing review. The teacher decides these can be addressed during the warm-up at the beginning of the lesson when the legs, arms, shoulders, and lower back muscles are prepared for the lesson activities. While students are warming up, the teacher uses this time to also address any issues related to the self-respect

Table 6.11 Sample Block Teaching Learning Map

Instruction Block 1: Ball Skills

Objectives/ days	Week 1					Week 2					Week 3					Week 4				
	M	T	W	T	F	M	T	W	T	F	M	T	W	T	F	M	T	W	T	F
Self-respect	O	O	O	O	O	O	O	O	O	O	O	O	O	O	O	O	O	O	O	O
Stretching	O	O	O	O	O	O	O	O	O	O	O	O	O	O	O	O	O	O	O	O
Warm-up	O	O	O	O	O	O	O	O	O	O	O	O	O	O	O	O	O	O	O	O
Fielding fly balls																				
Foot dribble		A	F	P	P	F	P	P	P	P	F	P	P	R						
Throw-in				A	F	F	P	P	P	P	F	P	P	P	R					
Hand dribble														A	F	P	P	P	R	
Two-hand chest pass						A	F	P	P	P	F	P	P	P	P	R				
Bounce pass							A	F	P	P	F	P	P	P	P	P	R			

Matrix Codes:

A = initial assessment

F = formal instruction

P = practice with ongoing assessment

O = ongoing application with review as needed

R = formal reassessment

Table 6.12 Sample Lesson Outline Based on BTLM

Lesson introduction	Warm-up—focus on leg, arm, shoulder, and lower back muscles Address any issues related to self-respect objective. Review focal points of foot dribble and throw-in objectives.
Lesson body	Introduce and demonstrate focal points of the two-hand chest pass. Divided students into instruction groups based on their assessment data. Set gym up into four instruction stations focusing on: 1. Foot dribble 2. Throw-in 3. Two-hand chest pass 4. Bounce pass While students practice at stations 1-3, the teacher assesses them on the bounce pass as they pass through station 4.
Lesson summary	Large-group game involving the two-hand chest pass Review the focal points of the two-hand chest pass.

objective that might require review and to review the focal points of the foot dribble and throw-in objectives. These objectives were assessed and formally taught during the previous week. The focus of the lesson body for this lesson is on the two-hand chest pass. The teacher demonstrates the focal points for this objective and emphasizes which focal points will be highlighted in today's lesson and how they are to be worked on at the two-hand chest pass station. Students are then divided into instructional groups based on their previous assessment data and are assigned to start work at one of the four instruction stations set up in the gym. One station focuses on the two-hand chest pass that was just explained to the class. Two of the other stations were introduced in the previous classes and focus on the foot dribble and throw-in. The final station is an assessment station in which the teacher will be positioned to assess the students' entry-level performance on the bounce pass objective. The teacher finishes the class with a large-group activity involving the two-hand chest pass and concludes this activity with a quick review of the focal points for the two-hand chest pass.

Initially, the sample Highland YTLMs and BTLMs might appear complicated and a bit intimidating. However, after you have created a few of these tables you will find them easier to create and use. Remember that most elementary physical education programs will not have the luxury of the Highland schools and be able to work on so many objectives. If your program has physical education only twice a week, you will be managing only about 40 percent of the amount of content shown in the Highland YTLMs and BTLMs. Creating the YTLMs and BTLMs gives teachers two major advantages. First, they capture the knowledge and experience of multiple teachers that participate in their creation so that information can be used by all teachers delivering the program. Second, once these plans are created, all teachers have a framework in place for future lesson planning. Now all they need to do is assess their students and individualize the lessons within these frameworks to address the unique needs of their students.

SUMMARY

We have looked at the initial elementary physical education program plan created by the Highland elementary physical educators using the ABC planning process. This plan should be viewed as the foundation for the start of an ongoing and dynamic process. The curriculum is based on the Highland teachers' best educational estimates for a host of variables. When they implement their curriculum these estimates can be validated or revised as needed based on program evaluation. For more detail on the ABC planning steps, review chapter 1 and consult Kelly and Melograno's *Developing the Physcial Education Curriculum* (2004) on the ABC model.

CHAPTER 7

USING THE *EVERYONE CAN!* ONLINE RESOURCE MATERIALS

In this chapter we describe how to access and use the extensive resource materials provided in the *Everyone Can* online resource at www.HumanKinetics.com/EveryoneCan. This resource collection is designed to be intuitive and easy to use. That said, we recommend that you take a few minutes to read this chapter so you can take full advantage of the *Everyone Can* resources.

HOW TO ACCESS THE *EVERYONE CAN* ONLINE RESOURCE

To access the *Everyone Can* resource materials you need Internet access and a Web browser such as Internet Explorer or Firefox. After you connect to the Internet and open your browser, enter the following URL: www.HumanKinetics.com/EveryoneCan. This takes you to the *Everyone Can* home page on the Human Kinetics Web site. Follow the instructions on the key code letter, just inside the book's front cover, to unlock the resource.

The *Everyone Can* online resource contains over 2,000 pages of instructional resource materials to assist you in meeting the physical education needs of your students. To help you quickly find what you are looking for, there are several ways to view various lists of resource materials. First, we will explore the main list viewing options and then we will examine each of the instructional resource materials in detail.

Finding Materials Related to an Objective

A typical way to find materials is to select a specific objective and view all of the materials related to that objective. The *Everyone Can* online resource allows you to type any part of an objective's name and then select the objective from a list of objectives that match what you typed. For example, if you wanted to view materials related to the overhand throw, you can start typing the word "throw." As you type, a list of objectives matching your input appears, and you can click the exact one you want. You will then see a list of all materials for that objective. Each objective has the same types of materials, which are described in more detail in the Exploring Instructional Resources section that follows. You can delimit your search by first selecting one of the Everyone Can goal areas from the dropdown list. You can also click on the "see the whole list" link to see an alphabetical list of all the objectives.

Finding Games by Name or by Goal

Another way to use the *Everyone Can* online resource is to find games either by name or related to a specific goal. To find games, first choose to view only games instead of all resource types under resources. You will see an alphabetical list of all games. If you start to type the name of a game in the area provided, the list will shrink to include only those games that match what you have typed. You can also delimit the list of games shown to one of the *Everyone Can* goals (e.g., body control or locomotor objectives) by first selecting a goal from the dropdown goal list.

Finding Games by Instructional Activity

Because games are most commonly used in *Everyone Can* to complement instruction on focal points of objectives, games have been coded to all instructional activities. The typical process would be to first select the objective and then the instructional activity for the focal point you want to teach, read through the activity to find the games that have been coded to that instructional activity, and then look up those games as previously described.

Finding Templates and Worksheets

The *Everyone Can* online resource includes templates and worksheets related to the instructional resources. The templates are blank forms corresponding to each of the instructional resources such as assessment items, assessment activities, games, posters, and so on. These templates can be used to do the chapter enrichment activities and to develop your own curricula and instructional materials. The worksheets that are used in the examples in the book and in many of the enrichment activities such as Program Goal Emphasis or Calculating Instructional Time. All the forms are provided as Word files so you can easily adapt them to suit your needs. To find a template or worksheet, select templates/worksheets under the resource type, and you will then receive a list of all the available forms. Click on the form you want, and it will open in Word.

EXPLORING THE INSTRUCTION MATERIALS

You should now understand how to access the various resource materials. We are now going to look at an example of the resource materials available for all the *Everyone Can* objectives. The resource materials are designed around the skill

levels and focal points of the 70 objective assessment items supplied in the online resource. You are provided one assessment item, an assessing activity, one disability accommodations sheet, two scoresheets, and one poster for each objective. In addition, you are provided with teacher instructional activities, station task cards, and large- and small-group games for every focal point of each objective assessment item. Let's look at a sample of the resource materials for the overhand throw (figures 7.1-7.7). We know the overhand throw is an object control skill, so we click on Object Control under the Goals menu on the home page. This displays a list of the object control skills. We then click on the overhand throw, which is the fourth objective on the list. Of course, we could have reached this same place typing overhand throw in the Objective control box. When you click on the overhand throw you are shown a list of all the resource materials available for this objective. Each item in the list is a link to the resource materials stored as PDF files. When you select a resource such as the assessment item for the overhand throw, your computer opens the program called Adobe Acrobat and then opens the file containing the assessment item into a new window so it can be displayed on your computer's screen. The text that follows shows a sample of each of the *Everyone Can* resources along with a brief explanation.

Objective Assessment Item

Assuming you selected the overhand throw and then clicked on the first resource, Assessment Item, you are now viewing the assessment item for the overhand throw. Review of the sample assessment item in figure 7.1 shows that each assessment item is divided into three sections. The first section composes the top of the form and tells you the name of the objective as well as the equipment and space required to administer this item. The second section of the assessment item is the definition of the skill levels down the left side of the form. The first skill level for all the assessment items, skill level 1, focuses on how the basic skill is performed. The second and third skill levels involve applications of skill level 1. For example, skill level 1 of the overhand throw focuses on mechanically throwing correctly, whereas skill levels 2 and 3 focus on the use of the skill level 1 pattern to throw for distance and accuracy, respectively. The third section of the assessment item is the definition of the focal points. Focal points are the critical performance criteria a student must demonstrate to perform the skill correctly. The skill level 1 focal points define specific performance criteria regarding how the skill is performed (e.g., feet apart, weight transfer, follow-through). For the overhand throw example shown in figure 7.1, students must demonstrate seven focal points on two of three trials in order to earn mastery of skill level 1. The skill level 2 and 3 focal points can be either additional performance criteria that is more advanced or, more commonly, product measures for distance and accuracy, as illustrated in the overhand throw example.

Assessment Activity

When you click on the second resource for any objective, you receive an assessment activity. The first part of the assessment activity form reviews the general instructions for conducting an assessment of the target objective. These instructions include administration reminders such as where to stand and what should be said to the students. They also remind the teacher to record students' ACE behaviors. The second part of the assessment activity provides instructions for how to involve students in an activity that allows the teacher to assess and

record student performance. The goal of all assessment activities is to involve students in an activity that is fun and engaging for students and that frees the teacher up to observe students on the objective being assessed (figure 7.2).

Disability Accommodations

When you click on the third resource for any objective, you receive a general list of disability accommodations. In most schools, most students with mild and moderate disabilities are included in the general physical education program. A

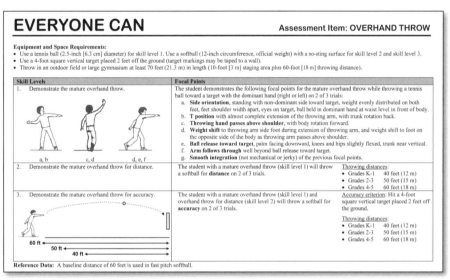

Figure 7.1   Objective assessment item for the overhand throw.

Illustrations reprinted from J. Wessel, 1976, *I can: Object control* (North Brook, IL: Hubbard Scientific Company), 35. By permission of J. Wessel.

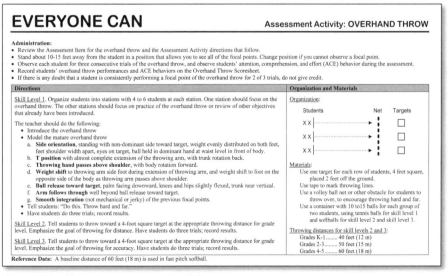

Figure 7.2   Sample assessment activity.

series of instructional guidelines are provided for teachers to assist them in accommodating the needs of students with developmental, sensory, and physical disabilities for each objective (figure 7.3).

Poster

When you click on the fourth resource for any objective, you receive a poster (figure 7.4), which is designed to be a visual aid for teachers and students. The poster can be printed and posted in the gym to remind students of the skill levels and focal points of the skills they are working on. Small copies of the posters can also be put on student task cards and given to students as handouts to take home.

Scoresheets

When you click on the fifth resource for any objective, you receive scoresheets. Two scoresheets are provided for each objective assessment item (figure 7.5). These scoresheets paraphrase the skill levels and focal points across the top of the columns and provide a row to enter each student's name and data. The first scoresheet is designed to be printed on standard letter paper and is the basic scoresheet for collecting student entry and exit performance data. The second scoresheet is the same as the first but contains evaluation columns on the right side. This scoresheet should be printed on legal paper (8.5 × 14 inches). The legal page can be folded into an 8.5-×-11-inch form, which will remove the evaluation columns until they are needed at the end of the instruction block or year. The scoresheets have been provided in an electronic format so teachers can modify them to meet their needs. For example, teachers can enter students' names with a word processing program or can change the scoring procedure from the X/O method to a scoring rubric.

Figure 7.3 Sample disability accommodation guidelines.

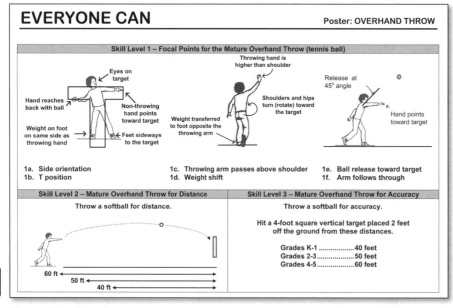

Figure 7.4 Sample poster.

Illustrations reprinted from J. Wessel, 1976, *I can: Object control* (North Brook, IL: Hubbard Scientific Company), 35. By permission of J. Wessel.

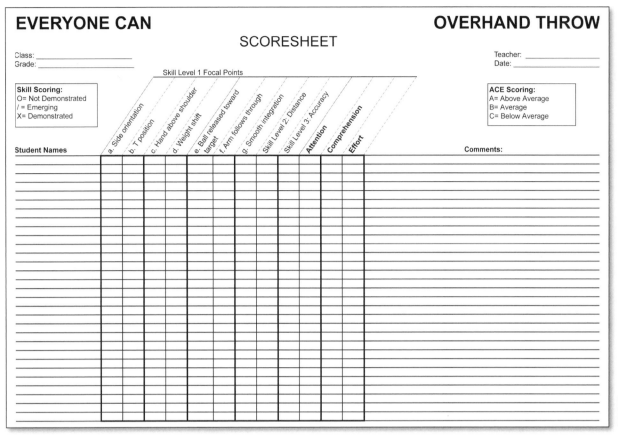

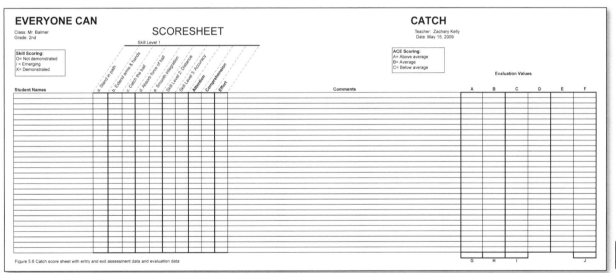

Figure 5.6 Catch score sheet with entry and exit assessment data and evaluation data

Figure 7.5 Sample scoresheets.

Teacher Instructional Activities

When you click on the sixth resource for any objective, you receive teacher instructional activities. These activities are designed specifically for teachers and summarize in a condensed format information on how to teach each focal point and skill level of the objective. The first page of the instructional activities for the catch performance objective is shown in figure 7.6. At the top of the form are general teaching recommendations and reminders specific to teaching this objective. A table is then shown that provides teachers with suggestions regarding organization, materials, activities, games, cues, and feedback that can be used when teaching each focal point and skill level of the objective. These are detailed descriptions that guide the teacher through how to prepare and organize the instructional setting, what to say to students, and how to provide feedback.

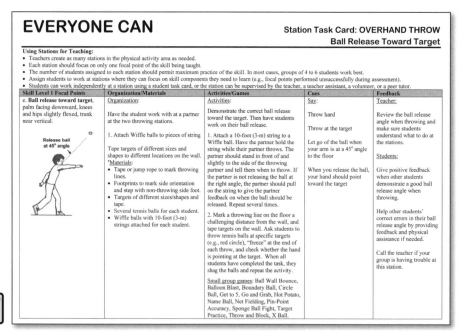

EVERYONE CAN Teaching Instructional Activities: OVERHAND THROW

Teaching the Overhand Throw:
• When the emphasis is on a specific focal point, the students should be practicing the focal point as an integrated part of the overhand throw.
• Use instructional cues that "paint a picture" or that describe the feel of the desired action. Make certain that students understand the instructional cues.
• Communicate the focus of instruction through demonstrations, station task cards, posters, or multiple methods.
• Design instruction so students receive feedback from the teacher, other students, and self-assessment.
• Use a variety of games and activities that emphasize the focal points.

Reminders:
• Maximize participation. Provide all students with many opportunities to practice. Have enough equipment for all students.
• Avoid elimination games. Students cannot practice if they do not participate in the activity.
• Minimize competition. When the emphasis shifts from playing to winning many students will regress back to their former immature movement patterns.

Skill Level 1 Focal Points	Organization/Materials	Activities/Games	Cues	Feedback
a. **Side orientation**, standing with non-dominant side toward target, weight evenly distributed on both feet, feet shoulder width apart, eyes on target, ball held in dominant hand at waist level in front of body.	Organization: / Throwing stations: / Teacher / Throwing relays: / XXXX / XXXX / XXXX / Materials: • Motivating targets. • Tape to mark throwing lines. • Footprints to mark side orientation. • Several tennis balls for each student.	Activities: / Demonstrate side orientation and then have the class perform the following activities: / *Throwing stations*: Create several stations with one or more students at a station. Use footprints to mark side orientation. Students throw toward targets on/near the gym walls. When all students finish throwing, students shag the balls and repeat the task. / *Throwing relays*: Create several stations with 3-4 students at a station. The student at the front of the line throws the ball, then takes a position at the back of the line. Other students provide feedback. Repeat the relay. / Small group games: Ball Wall Bounce, Balloon Blast, Boundary Ball, Circle Ball, Get to 5, Go and Grab, Hot Potato, Name Ball, Net Fielding, Pin-Point Accuracy, Sponge Ball Fight, Target Practice, Throw and Block, X Ball. / Large group games: Boundary Ball, Clean Out The Backyard, Leader Class, Sponge Ball Fight.	Say: / Stand sideways / Look at the target	Teacher: / Physically assist students having trouble so that they know what the correct side orientation position feels like. / Give positive feedback when students demonstrate the correct side orientation position. / Students: / Partners should give each other feedback on their side orientation position. / Give positive feedback when other students demonstrate the correct side orientation position.

Figure 7.6 Sample teacher instructional activity.

Illustrations reprinted from J. Wessel, 1976, *I can: Object control* (North Brook, IL: Hubbard Scientific Company), 35. By permission of J. Wessel.

EVERYONE CAN Station Task Card: OVERHAND THROW / Ball Release Toward Target

Using Stations for Teaching:
• Teachers create as many stations in the physical activity area as needed.
• Each station should focus on only one focal point of the skill being taught.
• The number of students assigned to each station should permit maximum practice of the skill. In most cases, groups of 4 to 6 students work best.
• Assign students to work at stations where they can focus on skill components they need to learn (e.g., focal points performed unsuccessfully during assessment).
• Students can work independently at a station using a student task card, or the station can be supervised by the teacher, a teacher assistant, a volunteer, or a peer tutor.

Skill Level 1 Focal Points	Organization/Materials	Activities/Games	Cues	Feedback
e. **Ball release toward target**, palm facing downward, knees and hips slightly flexed, trunk near vertical.	Organization: / Have the student work with at a partner at the two throwing stations. / 1. Attach Wiffle balls to pieces of string / Tape targets of different sizes and shapes to different locations on the wall. / Materials: • Tape or jump rope to mark throwing lines. • Footprints to mark side orientation and step with non-throwing side foot. • Targets of different sizes/shapes and tape. • Several tennis balls for each student. • Wiffle balls with 10-foot (3-m) strings attached for each student.	Activities: / Demonstrate the correct ball release toward the target. Then have students work on their ball release. / 1. Attach a 10-foot (3-m) string to a Wiffle ball. Have the partner hold the string while their partner throws. The partner should stand in front of and slightly to the side of the throwing partner and tell them when to throw. If the partner is not releasing the ball at the right angle, the partner should pull on the string to give the partner feedback on when the ball should be released. Repeat several times. / 2. Mark a throwing line on the floor a challenging distance from the wall, and tape targets on the wall. Ask students to throw tennis balls at specific targets (e.g., red circle), "freeze" at the end of each throw, and check whether the hand is pointing at the target. When all students have completed the task, they shag the balls and repeat the activity. / Small group games: Ball Wall Bounce, Balloon Blast, Boundary Ball, Circle Ball, Get to 5, Go and Grab, Hot Potato, Name Ball, Net Fielding, Pin-Point Accuracy, Sponge Ball Fight, Target Practice, Throw and Block, X Ball.	Say: / Throw hard / Throw at the target / Let go of the ball when your arm is at a 45° angle to the floor / When you release the ball, your hand should point toward the target	Teacher: / Review the ball release angle when throwing and make sure students understand what to do at the stations. / Students: / Give positive feedback when other students demonstrate a good ball release angle when throwing. / Help other students' correct errors in their ball release angle by providing feedback and physical assistance if needed. / Call the teacher if your group is having trouble at this station.

Figure 7.7 Sample station task card.

Illustration reprinted from J. Wessel, 1976, *I can: Object control* (North Brook, IL: Hubbard Scientific Company), 35. By permission of J. Wessel.

Station Task Cards

When you click on the seventh resource for any objective, you receive station task cards. These cards are provided for teachers who use a station approach for teaching. The station cards can be used by teachers to define and set up instruction stations. The station cards can also be used independently by upper-grade students who can read the cards. A sample station card is shown in figure 7.7. Each station card starts with a brief description of how the station can be used. The card then shows the focal point being addressed in the station, explains how to set up the stations, describes at least two sta-

ONLINE RESOURCE MATERIALS

tion activities, reviews pertinent cues, and finally describes how feedback should be given. These cards can be given to a TA or parent working with a student on a particular focal point. These materials can also be shared with families in your area who are homeschooling children to assist them in providing appropriate physical education.

Games

When you click on the last two resources for any objective, you receive a list of small and large group games. These are all of the small and large group games that have been recommended in the instructional activities for this objective. Remember, two small- and two large-group games are keyed to each focal point and skill level of each *Everyone Can* objective assessment item. A sample game is shown in figure 7.8. Each game card includes the object of the game, materials needed, how to organize the class, directions for playing the game, and suggested teaching alternatives. All games are given a physical activity rating that indicates whether the activity is easy, moderate, or vigorous. The typical procedure would be to select an instructional activity or station card for a given focal point of an objective and then to select a game to complement that activity. Once you know the name of the game you want, you go back to these resource lists and select that game from the list provided. Games can also be selected by choosing Games Only under the Resource Type on the *Everyone Can* home page and either searching for the name in the alphabetic list or typing the name of the game.

USING THE ONLINE RESOURCES

The *Everyone Can* resources can be used in many ways to help teachers organize and implement their instruction. A common method is to indicate in the teaching template (TT) for the lesson which *Everyone Can* resources will be used and then to include copies of these materials behind the TT in your teaching notebook. Page 53 shows a sample TT using this format. Note that the class information and managerial sections need to be filled out only once for each instruction block; they can then be copied and pasted for subsequent lessons.

A second common method of using the resources is to create a detailed teaching plan by inserting content from the *Everyone Can* resources into a teaching template or lesson plan. For example, let's say a teacher is working on teaching the overhand throw. Based on her assessment data, she has decided to focus instruction on the second focal point of the overhand throw—the T position. Table 7.1 shows a sample lesson plan in which content from the *Everyone Can* teacher instructional activities has been copied and pasted directly into the teaching plan. Let's examine how this was done. First, the teacher opened a blank teaching plan document in her word processing program. This document can be a simple self-made form, like the example shown, or you can use the more comprehensive blank teaching template provided under Forms in the *Everyone Can* online resource. The teacher entered information about the warm-up section of the lesson, but when she came to the lesson body section she decided she wanted to use some of the information from the *Everyone Can* resources materials.

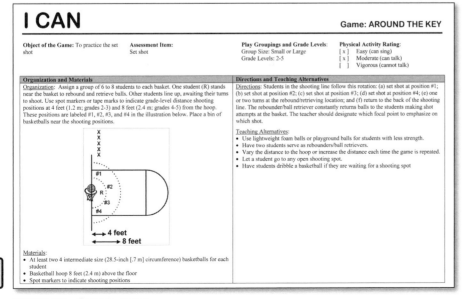

Figure 7.8 Sample game.

To do this she minimized her word-processing program (by clicking on the dash icon in the top right corner of the page, two icons to the left of the red X if you're in Word 2007). Minimizing a program keeps all the content active but temporarily clears the screen so another application can be used. The minimized program is shown at the bottom of the screen (in Word 2007). The teacher then opened her Web browser and connected to the *Everyone Can* home page. Because she was interested in information on the overhand throw, she clicked on Object Control under the Goal menu option and then clicked on Overhand Throw. Looking at the overhand throw main resource page, she then clicked on the PDF version of the teacher instructional activities. This action opened the Adobe Acrobat program and displayed instructional suggestions for each of the focal points and skill levels of the overhand throw. She scrolled down the list to skill level 1, focal point b, and found suggestions for demonstrat-

ing the T position. She then selected the Select Text option from the toolbar at the top of Adobe Acrobat, highlighted the content she wanted with her cursor, and clicked on Copy under the Edit menu. She then clicked on the icon for her word processing program at the bottom of the screen to redisplay her lesson plan form. She moved her cursor to the first column of the lesson body box and clicked on Paste under the Edit menu. This process transferred a copy of the text taken from the *Everyone Can* online resources into her lesson plan in her word processor.

Looking at table 7.1, you can see that this process was repeated for copying the student activity for the lesson body and for copying the picture shown under organization. What this example illustrates is that any content provided in the *Everyone Can* online resource can be copied and pasted into a lesson plan. While we hope this will encourage teachers to develop better and more detailed lesson plans, it is also important to give

Table 7.1   Sample Teaching Plan With Content Copied and Pasted From *Everyone Can*

Teacher: _____   Grade: _____   Start time: _____

Block #: _____   Start date: _____   End date: _____

Format/teacher	Student activity	Organization/equipment
Introduction		
Warm-up led by teacher	Students run 4 laps around the gym. Do sit and reach for 20 seconds. Do as many curl-ups as they can in 30 seconds. Do as many push-ups as they can in 30 seconds. While they warm up, the teacher reviews focal points of the overhand throw.	Run as a group
For exercises, scattered around gym in personal space
Lesson body		
Demonstrate the T position. Explain how the arms of the body make the crossbar of the T, and how the trunk of the body makes the stem of the T.	Create several stations with one or more students at a station. Place balls behind the student at waist level and have them reach back to grab a ball as they prepare to throw. Students throw toward targets on or near the gym walls. When all students finish throwing, students shag the balls and repeat the task.	5-6 paper balls or beanbags per student
Summary		
Teacher reviews focal points and emphasizes making a T before forward movement.	Divide the class into 4 teams by ability. Put the 2 higher ability teams on one court and the other 2 teams on another court. The goal of the game is to get as many balls as possible on the other team's court in 30 seconds.	Set up 2 nets and make 4 teams. Need 100 paper balls. Set the nets as high as possible.

The content in this document has been copied in whole or in part from Kelly, L.E., Wessel, J.A., Dummer, G., & Thompson, T. (2008). *Everyone Can: The elementary physical education skill development and assessment resource.* Champaign, IL: Human Kinetics.

proper credit for the source of any information copied form *Everyone Can*. To avoid any potential plagiarism or conflicts with copyright regulations, the following statement should be included on any document you create using the *Everyone Can* materials:

> From L.E. Kelly, J.A. Wessel, G.Dummer, & T. Sampson, 2010, *Everyone Can! Online Resource* (Champaign, IL: Human Kinetics).

This text can be copied and pasted to the bottom of each page of your documents, or you can insert it as a footer using your word processing program, and it will be automatically added to the bottom of each page. If you use any of the predefined forms supplied on the *Everyone Can* online resource, this footnote has already been created for you.

METHODS FOR PRINTING POSTERS

The default is to print the posters on standard 8.5-×-11-inch sheets of paper. This size is good for individual student use and also for aides and parents. For class use, teachers like to make larger posters. There are three options for making the posters larger. The first option is the easiest but also the most costly. You can print out an 8.5-×-11-inch copy or bring a file from the *Everyone Can* online resource to a local print shop that has a "large format" printer. Tell them what size you want, and they can print the poster. The second option is to use a standard printer and print the poster out as a series of tiles and then put the tiles together to make the large poster. To do this, you need a software program that supports this function, or you can buy a program designed to do so. Most major graphics design programs like Photoshop and CorelDRAW support this type of printing and are readily available in most schools. Examples of specialized programs that cost around $20 are Proposter and Digital Camera Poster Creator. Applications like these can be found by Googling "printing posters standard printer" on the Internet. It should be noted that because the original figures supplied in the *Everyone Can* materials are relatively small, they will begin to blur as the size of the poster is increased. The third option is to project the image of the poster onto mural paper taped to the wall and then trace the poster onto the paper. The image can be projected by using either a digital projector (used to show PowerPoint presentations) or converting the original image into an overhead and then using an overhead projector. This is the tried and true old-fashioned way, but it still works. This task can be turned into an art project for students or incorporated as a project in the school's before- or after-school program. The advantage of this third option is that you can make the posters whatever size you want by adjusting the distance of the projector from the wall. Some schools have used this technique and permanently painted the posters on the walls around the gym. The posters provided on the *Everyone Can* online resource are simple black-and-white drawings. Another advantage of options 2 and 3 are that you can color in the posters to make them more captivating.

OTHER USES FOR THE *EVERYONE CAN* RESOURCES

Although most teachers can get a few new ideas from the *Everyone Can* materials, many experienced teachers might feel they can plan adequately without them. Do not interpret this to mean that the *Everyone Can* materials are not a valuable resource for experienced teachers. One of the major advantages of the *Everyone Can* resource materials is that they can be used as resources for others who want to assist students in learning or practicing their motor skills. For example, it is not uncommon for parents or guardians to contact a physical educator and ask what they can do to help their child on a given skill. Because of time constraints faced by most physical educators, these requests are usually answered by giving the parents a few quick verbal suggestions. Though many physical educators would like to sit down and write up more substantive and individualized suggestions for parents, few find the time to do it. Using the *Everyone Can* materials and providing interested parents or guardians with detailed suggestions is an easy task. The key is to know exactly what the student needs to work on from your assessment data; you can then easily find information on the focal points the student needs to work on. You can selectively pick content from the teacher instructional activities, station cards, and games and print them out to share. Because the *Everyone Can* materials are so easy to reproduce and share with parents and guardians, you need to be careful not to overwhelm anyone with information. A few carefully selected resources based on the student's assessed needs are probably more helpful than 30+ pages of resources on an objective.

Among others who find *Everyone Can* resources helpful are classroom aides and volunteers. These individuals have the best of intentions but often know little about teaching motor skills to students. Ideally, physical educators would have time allocated in their schedules to train these volunteers and prepare them for the content to be taught. Unfortunately, this rarely occurs to the degree needed because of scheduling and other time constraints. So this is another time when *Everyone Can* resources come in handy. Teachers can look ahead in the BTLMs and discover what content will be addressed in upcoming classes. Volunteers can then be given information on objectives, activities, and games directly from *Everyone Can* in advance so they can review them before they are covered in class. Again, it would be ideal if time could be planned for you to meet with volunteers to discuss questions they have after reviewing the materials. While using the *Everyone Can* materials alone is no substitute for training and planning time with volunteers, they do provide a means of maximizing efficiency to help you make the most of the little time you have to prepare volunteers for working in your classes.

Elementary-aged students need activity. It is not uncommon for classroom teachers to seek input from physical educators for games to be played with the class during recess or at other times when kids seem to need to burn off extra energy. Ideally, you would recommend cooperative games that incorporate the skills you are currently working on in physical education that would keep students active while maximizing their on-task time and the number of practice trials they receive. In reality, teachers usually accept simple team games like kickball or tagging and fleeing games because it is too time consuming to explain more appropriate games and activities. With the *Everyone Can* resources, you can print off several games for other teachers that complement what you are teaching in physical education and provide the classroom teacher with all the necessary information to implement the game. Again, do not overwhelm teachers with too much information. Start out with one or two games and then give them more if they ask for it.

A special group of teachers you might frequently work with are instructional aides assigned to work with students with disabilities in physical education. Allot time in your schedule to meet with these aides and train them so they know what you will be covering in class and what they should be working on with their students with disabilities. You can use your BTLMs to show them what content will be worked on during the next instruction block and the *Everyone Can* resources related to their student's IEP to assist them in working with their students. The *Everyone Can* materials will surely help the aides provide better instruction, but they will still need you periodically to assess their students and advise them on how to revise instruction accordingly.

Finally, *Everyone Can* materials are valuable resources to share with families in your community who are homeschooling children. In these cases, it would probably be best for them to purchase *Everyone Can* themselves and then to meet with you for guidance on how to best use the materials. When you meet with homeschoolers, you would share with them your school's achievement-based curriculum. It would also be a good idea to give them copies of your curriculum scope and sequence chart, the YTLMs and BTLMs. With these materials in hand, you could show them how to use *Everyone Can* to plan and implement a home physical education program for their children.

USING *EVERYONE CAN* FOR INDIVIDUALIZED EDUCATION PROGRAMS

Today, many children with mild and moderate disabilities receive their physical education in the general physical education program. This means that the general physical education teacher might be called on to create individualized educational programs (IEPs) for students when an adapted physical educator is not available. *Everyone Can* is a valuable tool for assisting you in creating IEPs.

First, you will be asked to assess and report the students' present level of performance. This can be determined by conducting a general needs assessment, as described in chapter 2, in which you assess students with disabilities on the objectives targeted for instruction in the preceding and coming years in your physical education curriculum as shown in the curriculum scope and sequence chart using *Everyone Can's* objective assessment instruments. Based on your assessment results, the degree of delay, and the learning characteristics of the students that have been assessed, you then define long-term goals and short-term instructional objectives for each student. For many students with mild disabilities, their goals might be to master the same objectives identified in the curriculum for the other students. They might only need some accommodations to help them attend during instruction or stay on task during practice. Students with more severe disabilities might need to work on fewer objectives. If general students are working on mastering eight locomotor skills over their six years in the program, a student with a severe disability who learns at a slower rate might be targeted to master four locomotor skills over the same time period.

Once you determine goals for these students, which are the objectives they will be working on mastering that year, the next task is to define short-term instructional objectives. The short-term objectives are a sequence of smaller learning tasks that lead to the attainment of each of the IEP goals. Using the *Everyone Can* objective assessment items, the short-term instructional objectives become the focal points the student needs to master for the skill targeted as the goal. As discussed in chapter 2, it might be necessary when working with some students with more severe disabilities to further break down the *Everyone Can* focal points for a given skill into smaller learning steps. Most schools have established forms for IEPs. You should be able to obtain electronic versions of these forms and then cut and paste *Everyone Can* materials into the form, as described previously for making teaching templates. An additional advantage of using the *Everyone Can* materials is that you can duplicate the instruction materials for the focal points you are working on and share them with teacher aides and the student's family so they know exactly what you are working on and can reinforce your instruction. Take care not to overwhelm anyone with too much material, but encourage them to work with their child. Most children with disabilities need many practice trials outside of physical education to develop their motor skills, and parents or guardians can be a valuable resource.

SUMMARY

You should now have a good understanding of the breadth of the *Everyone Can* online resource materials and how they can be used to assist you in addressing the physical education needs of your students. The *Everyone Can* materials have the potential to increase your teaching effectiveness and the achievement of your students. However, to harness these benefits requires a small investment of your time to learn how to use the materials and then to integrate them into your daily teaching.

CHAPTER 8

INCORPORATING THE ABC MODEL INTO YOUR PROGRAM

Becoming an effective teacher is a lifelong pursuit. Many teachers find the longer they teach, the more exciting and challenging teaching becomes. Though the managerial aspects of the job become easier over time, once you have established your rules and routines, the challenge of efficiently teaching so that *every* student in your program achieves the objectives in your curriculum in the time available is a never-ending quest. Unfortunately, many teachers pursue this quest of teaching excellence on their own. One of the goals of the ABC model is to provide teachers with a means of combining and sharing their efforts. In this chapter we offer suggestions for how the ABC model and *Everyone Can* resources can be used for in-service training in physical education. It would be ideal for all the physical education staff to participate in these work sessions, but most of the suggestions can also be implemented individually or by small groups of teachers.

In many districts, in-service training is haphazard and poorly planned and implemented in physical education. Time is set aside in the district calendar for a few days of in-service each year, but many teachers do not find these presentations helpful because they are too general and do not apply to their needs. Most teachers quickly learn that in-service training offers no magical solutions. This is not to say you cannot be inspired or learn some new techniques at in-services, but in most cases designing and implementing solutions to address significant issues requires much more than a two- to three-hour workshop.

What we propose is using the ABC model and the talents of your teaching staff to address your own in-service needs. All teachers bring unique talents and experiences to the job. They also have teaching strengths and weaknesses. For example, we all have some motor skills we can easily teach to any student and other skills we find more difficult to teach. A goal then is to create an in-service program that enables teachers to share their talents while not threatening them or making them feel defensive. It is not uncommon for the vast majority of in-service needs identified by teachers to be addressed through this approach either through formal training sessions, such as in-services conducted by other teachers, or through more informal mechanisms, such as mentoring programs, in which teachers are paired to work with each other. Occasionally, a need arises in which a physical education staff can benefit from the talents of an outside expert to address a certain problem or issue. The difference here is that these requests for in-services are based on the needs of the physical education staff and targeted at a specific need.

DESIGNING AN IN-SERVICE PROGRAM

The first step in designing an in-service program is to conduct a needs assessment to determine to what degree your current program can answer four questions:

1. What content will be taught to each grade, and when will it be achieved by *all* students?

2. Where are the students on the content scheduled for instruction, and what do they need to learn next?

3. How is instruction designed and implemented to address identified needs of the students?

4. Is the curriculum working—are all students leaving the program with mastery of all program objectives?

This needs assessment can be conducted through a variety of methods, such as surveying all physical education teachers or via a staff meeting in which these questions are addressed by the group. What will immediately become clear is that there will always be a list of issues under each of these questions—areas in which improvements can be made. So it is usually necessary to list all needs identified during needs assessment and rank them in order of importance. The top two or three become the focus of in-service efforts for the year.

If you and your staff are just beginning to use the ABC model, the issues and problems will probably parallel the five components of the ABC model. That is, there will initially be concerns regarding the content of the curriculum—what content should be taught and when it should be mastered. Once an ABC plan is defined and refined, the needs generally shift to assessing and implementation issues. Finally, as teachers become more familiar and competent implementing their ABC curriculum, the focus shifts to issues related to student and program evaluation and program dissemination.

The purpose of this section is to illustrate how these questions can be used to guide in-service sessions for physical education. The four questions just posed will be used as an outline and ideas will be presented on how these topics can be addressed by capitalizing on the strengths of the physical education staff.

QUESTION 1: What content will be taught each year, and when will it be achieved by *all* students?

The ABC program-planning steps presented in chapter 1 can be used to guide a physical education staff through the process of creating a functional physical education program. Remember the ABC model is a process. It does not dictate what content is to be included in the curriculum, when it should be taught or mastered, or how it is to be taught. What the ABC model does is provide a process to guide you and fellow teachers through a series of steps that allow you to decide what content to include in your curriculum, when it will be taught, and when it will be achieved (table 8.1). A model curriculum was described in chapter 6 to provide a concrete example of the program-planning steps. Because the needs, resources, and students of every district are unique, there is no perfect curriculum for school districts to adopt. Each physical education curriculum must be created by teachers who will implement it and be designed around unique needs and resources. For example, your district might have physical education only twice a week for 30 minutes instead of five times a week as in the model curriculum. In this case, your staff would need to reduce the number of objectives included in your program based on time constraints. The model curriculum is also complemented by an extensive set of resources to assist you in assessing and teaching 70 of the most common objectives taught in elementary physical education. Again, these materials are provided as

Table 8.1   ABC Program Planning

Step	Purpose	Action
1.	Philosophy, goals, and objectives	Modify to address local needs
2.	Goal emphasis and number of objectives	List and re-rank
3.	Calculate instruction and mastery times	Recalculate based on local resources
4.	Determine number of objectives per goal	Based on local time constraints
5.	Program scope and sequence	Resequence
6.	Create teaching learning maps	Developed by teachers

examples. We hope many of them can be used as they are to address your needs. In some cases, the materials might need to be modified or new materials be created. In these situations you are encouraged to adapt the existing *Everyone Can* materials or to use them as models for developing your own content.

Preferably, ABC planning steps 1 through 5 (see chapter 1) should be done with the involvement of the entire physical education staff or, if not by all, by as many as possible via a series of in-service workshops. Once the scope and sequence of the curriculum is defined (step 5), the development of the yearly and block teaching and learning maps can be developed by small groups of teachers and shared with the group. The planning workshops should be spread across an entire year to allow time to consider and discuss the content between sessions and so that the amount of work is distributed over time.

Once the ABC curriculum is created, it is important to be realistic about how it is implemented. In many cases implementing an ABC curriculum requires a lot of change on the part of physical educators. We recommend that the curriculum be implemented on a small scale initially to allow teachers time to adjust their teaching. A common method is for teachers to start by implementing the curriculum in one class, usually at the lowest grade level they teach. When they feel comfortable implementing all aspects of the model (i.e., assessing, implementation planning, teaching, and evaluation) with one class, they can add classes until they are implementing the model for all their classes at that grade level. Finally, they add the next grade level as students from the initial grade level progress through the program. Again, there is no magic system. What is most important is that teachers progress at a rate that is both manageable and successful.

QUESTION 2: Where are the students on the content scheduled for instruction, and what do they need to learn next?

Using the ABC model, these questions are answered by assessing students on the objectives targeted for instruction (see chapter 2) and analyzing the assessment data to determine which focal points need to be addressed during instruction. The challenge here is not in knowing what should be done but in having the skill to do it. Assessing is typically one of the more stressful elements of learning to use the ABC model. This is true for two reasons. First, assessment is a change. Teachers are being asked to do something different. Second, assessment is threatening. The assumption is that given the assessment items and the rationale for assessing, all teachers need to do is to start assessing. But assessing is complicated, especially if you have not been trained in this mode of assessment or have not done it for years. Learning to assess motor skills using criterion-referenced items such as the *Everyone Can* assessment items is a two-step process. Teachers first learn and internalize the skill levels and focal points for the objectives they are assessing so they can observe them without having to refer to the prompts on the scoresheet between each observation. Second, they practice observing these focal points under controlled conditions in which they can receive feedback on the accuracy of their judgments. Learning the focal points is not difficult but does take time and practice. Trying to learn too many objectives at one time can be overwhelming. We recommend that teachers start with objectives targeted for mastery for the lowest grade level they teach. Once these objectives have been mastered, they progress to working on the objectives in the subsequent grades until they are all mastered. Once focal points have been memorized, teachers must learn to accurately observe them. This can be the most time-consuming and threatening aspect of learning to assess. For this phase, teachers must have access to immediate feedback. In other words, after they observe a performance of a skill and judge whether a focal point was demonstrated or not, they need to know whether this judgment was correct. The two most common methods for developing this skill are for the teacher to work with an expert or to use a video of performances that have already been assessed and scored by an expert. The advantage of using the expert model is that in addition to giving feedback on whether the judgment was correct, the expert can provide an explanation. The disadvantages of the expert model are that teachers can learn and practice only when they have access to the expert, and performing in front of an expert can be very stressful. The video method has the advantage that it can be used independently by teachers whenever they have time to practice. The major shortcoming of the video method is that it tells teachers only whether their judgments are correct or not and allows no discussion.

When designing in-service workshops to focus on assessing, a variety of options should be considered to allow for different learning styles. Some teachers prefer an individual process in which they can learn on their own, whereas other teachers prefer to practice in small groups in which they can discuss their performance with others. Teachers learning to assess have four requirements. They need . . .

1. an assessment item for the objective,

2. a scoring method,

3. video clips of students performing the target objective at different ability levels, and

4. expert evaluation of the video clips.

The *Everyone Can* online resource provides an assessment item for 70 of the most common objectives taught in elementary physical education. Although it is anticipated that these assessment items will be applicable in the form provided for most physical education settings, teachers do have the option of copying the items and modifying them to meet their needs. For example, teachers can copy the focal points of a given objective to their own document and then choose to add additional focal points or remove or combine one or more focal points. Teachers might also determine in their planning process that they want to include an objective in their curriculum that is not included in the 70 provided by *Everyone Can*. In this case, the teachers will need to find an assessment item for this objective in the literature or create their own assessment item. If they choose to create their own, they can use the *Everyone Can* items as models and the assessment item template provided in the online resource to create their new items.

The second prerequisite for learning to assess is a scoring and recording method. *Everyone Can* provides a scoresheet for each objective assessment item that incorporates a simple X/O scoring method. As discussed in chapter 2, there are many

other scoring methods. If a different method will be used, it needs to be defined and scoresheets developed for each objective. Then all teachers on the staff need to be trained on how to use this method. Again, a template is provided in the online resource for the *Everyone Can* scoresheet; it can be modified to meet your needs.

Once assessment items and scoresheets have been established, the next step is to create a video library for the objectives in your curriculum. Making the videos is relatively simple. Teachers can be assigned different objectives and then record their students performing these skills. They should ensure that a wide range of skill levels be included on each video. This can usually be accomplished by recording students in the grade levels below and above the level for which the objective is targeted for mastery in the curriculum.

The last step is to develop an answer key for each of the videos. Hiring an expert to assess the performances on the video is the best solution but might be too expensive. A second option is to develop a composite answer key by having the staff evaluate the clips and then review and discuss them until consensus is reached. The staff might be divided into groups of five or six to distribute this work. We recommend that the teacher of the students on the video not be involved in the evaluation.

Understand that when you use the staff-evaluation method, the peer group doing the evaluating tends to be more liberal than conservative in their ratings. They should remember that when in doubt about a student mastering a focal point, they should not give credit. If you do not give the student credit during assessment, the student will continue to work on the focal point. But if you erroneously give students credit for a focal point they do not have, they will not receive further instruction on this component and will continue to fail until they are reassessed.

Once assessment videos and the scoring key have been developed, they can be checked out and used by teachers as needed. Although developing videos and scoring keys might sound like an overwhelming task, it can be done over time. An elementary school physical education program that has physical education twice a week for 30 minutes would have only 24 to 30 objectives in their curriculum. The physical education staff could start by developing videos and scoring keys for the four or five objectives targeted for mastery in kindergarten the first year. Then each subsequent year they could make videos and keys for remaining objectives until after six years they have videos for each objective in their curriculum.

QUESTION 3: How is instruction designed and implemented to address the identified needs of the students?

We cannot emphasize enough that although *Everyone Can* is a powerful resource that will assist you with your physical education instruction, it is how you use the materials that makes the difference. What you have been provided is a model curriculum and some great ideas for assessing and teaching 70 of the most common objectives taught in elementary physical education. That said, it should be understood that there is no one single way to optimally teach every student any given physical education objective. The true talent of teaching is your ability to assess the learning needs of your students and then to create optimal teaching cues, instruction activities, and games that address their needs and help them learn the skill being taught.

Everyone Can gives you a foundation of ideas, methods, activities, and games. As you teach your students over your career, you will create hundreds of other unique teaching cues, games, and instructional activities. One of the tragedies of our profession is that we have limited ways to capture this wealth of material created over our careers. What happens in most cases is when we retire we take our great ideas with us, and the next teacher hired must rediscover or reinvent them all over again.

In chapter 3 (Implementation Planning), we recommended that teachers organize their teaching learning maps, assessment scoresheets, teaching templates, and associated materials (e.g., station cards, game cards etc.) into a notebook. This method provides a written record of what was taught in each class and also provides a means of evaluative commentary to be recorded and used to revise teaching methods in the future. In chapter 7 you were shown how to use the *Everyone Can* materials in conjunction with a teaching tem-

plate form provided on the *Everyone Can* online resource to create word-processed plans for your teaching. The major advantage of these methods is they provide a foundation on which you can build in teaching these objectives year after year. The assessed needs of each group of students will change from year to year, but you will have ready access to instructional strategies that you have used with success in the past. Instead of reinventing lessons each year, you can start with them and either refine of expand on them to better meet the needs of your next group of students. The advantage of having your teaching templates and *Everyone Can* resources in electronic format is that you can easily make these changes by cutting and pasting the content.

Once you begin developing your implementation materials electronically, we would like to provide a way to capture these ideas or any modifications you have made to the *Everyone Can* materials so that they can be shared with others. To assist you in capturing these ideas and making a permanent record of them in your physical education curriculum, we have created blank templates for each of the *Everyone Can* components, including assessment items, instruction activities, games, and so on. These templates are provided on the online resource and can be used to record your teaching materials so you can share them with fellow teachers and eventually pass them on to the teacher who replaces you. Figure 8.1 shows the template for an *Everyone Can* game. You can open the template using your Adobe program. Replace the prompts with your content and save the file with a name that describes the game you have created.

In addition to helping you share your ideas with colleagues, we would also like to create a way for the best of these ideas to be included in future editions of *Everyone Can*. Yes, there are limitations to how much content we can include in future editions, but we would like to provide you with a forum to share your most successful ideas with us and perhaps have them published among the best of the best. If you think you have created materials we should consider for our next edition, please enter them on the blank templates in the online resource and submit them to us for consideration. If your idea is selected, we would of course credit you as the author.

I CAN

Game: Enter Name

Object of the Game:
State the goal of the game.

Performance Objectives:
List the objective or objectives this game can be used to reinforce.

Play Groupings and Age:
Indicate whether it is a large or small group game and age range.

Physical Activity Rating: Check one
[   ] Easy
[   ] Moderate
[   ] Vigorous

Organization and Materials	Directions and Teaching Alternatives
Organization: Describe how the class should be organized to play this game as well as how any equipment should be setup. Provide an illustration when appropriate Materials: List the materials needed to play this game	Directions: Provide specific instructions on how the game is played and how it should be introduced to the students. Teaching Alternatives: 1. List at least 3 ways the game can be modified or played other ways.

Figure 8.1 *Everyone Can* game template.

We are also open to ideas of ways we can improve or expand on the *Everyone Can* materials. If you have an idea that does not fit one of our templates, or if you have created a unique scoresheet, a cumulative progress chart, or have some other clever ideas, you can also submit them for consideration. If we like your idea, we will give you credit and include your creation in our next edition. To submit your ideas, send them to E1canelem@gmail.com. Please note that this is a receive-mail-only account. When a message is sent to this account, you will receive an automated response. Periodically, all of the messages in the account will be downloaded and reviewed. Once we have determined how often the *Everyone Can* online resource can be updated, a review schedule will be established and you will be informed of the status of your submission.

QUESTION 4: Is the curriculum working—are all students leaving the program with mastery of all the program objectives?

There is much attention today on standards-based education in K-12 schools. This has increased the demand on schools to be more accountable, which in turn has increased demands on instruction time. For physical education to retain its current instruction time, it needs to be able to communicate and justify both the benefits of physical education for students and that the students are leaving physical education having achieved these benefits. Unfortunately, many parents judge physical education based on the experiences they had when they were in physical education and not on the merits of their children's current physical education program. This being the case, we need to work collectively with colleagues to develop a public information program for physical education so parents have a clear understanding of the goals and objectives of our physical education programs and where their children are on achieving them.

The ABC model provides a solid infrastructure for both student and program evaluation. The program philosophy statement communicates the overall benefits of the physical education program, and the program scope and sequence shows how these benefits are achieved by stipulating when each objective in the curriculum is taught and when it will be achieved. The curriculum scope and sequence is complemented by YTLMs and BTLMs, which delineate when students are assessed, taught, and evaluated on the content. These maps are further supported by teaching notebooks and teaching templates that detail how the content was actually delivered. The challenge for the physical education staff is managing all this information so it can be used both to improve the program and communicate its effectiveness to others.

Before initiating a public information program for your physical education program, we recommend that you first establish the program is in fact effective. Are most students leaving the program having achieved its stated goals and objectives? Many teachers assume this is the case for their programs, but they do not have the data to back it up. With the ABC model in place, you will have the data you need because it is collected as an integral part of the ABC teaching process via the students' entry and exit assessment performance scores. The challenge, as discussed in chapters 2 and 5, is computerizing these data so they can be quickly accessed and analyzed to evaluate the overall effectiveness of your program. Figure 8.2 shows an evaluation report that summarizes the average percentage mastery of students for four common locomotor skills across all elementary schools in a district. This figure was generated with a database management program that calculated each student's percentage mastery for each locomotor objective by dividing their exit score by the mastery criteria for the objective (i.e., the number of focal points in skill level 1). The shaded cells in the figure indicate when objectives were targeted to be achieved in this curriculum. Examination of data reveals that for the run, gallop, and hop, physical educators appear to be doing an excellent job, with nearly 100 percent of students demonstrating mastery during the year the objectives were targeted to be achieved. However, there appears to be a problem with the skip. By the end of second grade, only 75.6 percent of students have achieved mastery on the skip. This could mean teachers need help in better teaching the skip or that students need more time to learn this objective and it should be targeted for mastery later in the curriculum. The point here is that once you have data you can use

FIGURE 8.2
Sample report of average percentage of mastery by grade and objective.

Report date: May 2, 2007

Total number of students: 1,762

Objectives	Grades					
	K	1	2	3	4	5
Run	98.2	100.0	100.0	100.0	100.0	100.0
Hop	77.6	90.7	98.3	100.0	100.0	100.0
Gallop	72.3	92.4	99.1	100.0	100.0	100.0
Slide	68.5	89.4	96.9	100.0	100.0	100.0
Skip	25.8	49.6	75.6	94.8	100.0	100.0

Mastery targets are shaded.

Reprinted, by permission, from L.E. Kelly and V.J. Melograno, 2004, *Developing the physical education curriculum: An achievement-based approach* (Champaign, IL: Human Kinetics), 268.

it to see how effective your program is and then make changes as needed so you can document the program's success.

As addressed under the first three needs assessment questions in this chapter, the goal is to develop a practical approach to program evaluation that can realistically be implemented by the teachers in your school. As mentioned, we recommend that you start small and proceed with small steps. Assuming that you and your fellow teachers cannot immediately computerize all your student data, you could start by having all teachers collect and enter the entry and exit performance scores for just one class—preferably starting with their lowest grade: kindergarten. The next year, teachers would continue the process with a new kindergarten class and add entering data on one first-grade class. The process would continue until data were being entered each year for one class per grade level. With just these data, you could evaluate the effectiveness of your program over time based on the performance of the students in these sample classes. As instructor ability to collect, record, and enter assessment data increases, more and more data can be entered each year until all student data are on the computer.

Once you have established a workable evaluation process for your school district and are consistently showing positive results—students are achieving the grade and program objectives on schedule—you are ready to begin publicizing your program. This can start simple with computerized student progress reports being sent home each marking period and with a summary report sent home at the end of the year reporting students' overall progress. The physical education staff could also begin to give annual reports to the school's central administration and school board, documenting their effectiveness in meeting the program's goals. Once the physical education entry and exit student performance data are entered into a computerized database, any number of reports and graphs can be made to document the program's effectiveness. The staff could review these options and decide which reports should be generated each year and who they should be shared with. Assignments could then be distributed across the staff so that each staff member, or small groups of staff, is responsible for generating a part of the overall reports needed each year.

MANAGING CHANGE

It is not uncommon for members of a physical education staff to agree that there is a problem with their physical education curriculum and that something needs to be changed. The challenge is coming up with a solution that everyone agrees on and then devoting time and energy to implementing the solution. The ABC model provides a systematic process for guiding a physical education staff through a collaborative process of designing a functional physical education curriculum that is acceptable to everyone. The model curriculum in chapter 6 and the *Everyone Can* resource materials facilitate the process by reducing the amount of time needed to get started. However, having the perfectly defined curriculum and the world's best resource materials are of no value if they are not implemented. The major challenge of any curriculum revision process is change. Change often involves an element of risk and usually requires additional effort. Unfortunately, in education there are usually no extrinsic reinforcers (e.g., more pay for changing), leaving intrinsic rewards (e.g., student success and self-satisfaction) as the primary motivators. Though one would hope these intrinsic rewards would be enough, they must compete with all the other inequities involved in teaching (e.g., low pay, lack of respect, overcrowded classes, etc.). On top of this, there is still the possibility that if you take the risk and try to teach a new way you could still fail.

There is no magic solution to the problem of change. Changing your teaching behavior is comparable to students learning new motor skills. Many students *want* to be able to perform motor skills they cannot perform, but their desire is not enough for them to learn the skills. What they need is practice, feedback, and success. Although understanding what aspects of your teaching need to change and having a positive attitude are good prerequisites for change, change will only occur after you take the risk and try the new teaching method. Just as is true for your students, for change to work, you need practice, feedback, and success. The challenge for many elementary physical educators is getting feedback so they can be successful. One solution is to develop a mentoring system within your district and use in-service time to release teachers so they can observe each other and give each other feedback. Another option is to record your own teaching and then to review and discuss the video with a colleague. The bottom line is that for change to occur teachers need to be placed in an environment where they feel comfortable taking a risk and in which they are provided positive, constructive feedback that allows them to experience success. Although some of these points are common sense, here are some other considerations:

1. Accept that change is hard and might be more difficult for some teachers than others.

2. Everyone needs success to change, and some teachers need more success than others.

3. It is hard to change many teaching behaviors on your own without feedback.

4. Partners and small groups can be helpful if trained to focus on the positive and not compete.

5. Avoid the temptation to try to change too much too fast. Take baby steps and go slow.

6. Share your successes.

The bottom line is that no one else is going to redesign your curriculum, collect student performance data, computerize it, and analyze it for you to evaluate the effectiveness of your physical education curriculum and your ability to implement it. You have to do it yourself.

SUMMARY

There are increasing demands on schools to be more accountable. Many states have established performance standards that schools must achieve in order to be accredited. These programs are increasing the demands for more instruction time in the traditional academic areas of reading, math, and language arts. It is up to the members of the physical education staff to develop a plan that they can implement and that will produce the results needed to document their program effectiveness and justify the amount of time allocated to physical education in the school curriculum. Fortunately, there is also increasing public awareness of the need for children to be more physically active and of the health risks associated with obesity and inactivity. This suggests that most parents would probably support physical education as long as they understood the goals and benefits of the program and were confident students were leaving the program with these benefits. Your mission is to develop and nurture this community and parent support for your physical education program. The ABC model and *Everyone Can* materials are provided to assist you in fulfilling this mission.

References and Resources

Block, M.E. (2000). *Including students with disabilities in general physical education* (2nd ed.). Baltimore: Brooks.

Brandt, R.S. (Ed.). (2000). *Education in a new era.* Alexandria, VA: ASCD.

Burk, M.C. (2002). *Station games.* Champaign, IL: Human Kinetics.

Byl, J. (2002). *Co-ed recreational games.* Champaign, IL: Human Kinetics.

Byl, J. (2004). *101 Fun warm-up and cool-down games.* Champaign, IL: Human Kinetics.

Carpenter, J. (2007). *Physical education self-management for healthy, active lifestyles.* Champaign, IL: Human Kinetics.

Centers for Disease Control and Prevention (CDC). (2007). Overweight and obesity. www.cdc.gov/nccdphp/dnpa/obesity/index.htm.

Centers for Disease Control and Prevention (CDC). (2003). Physical activity levels among children aged 9-13 years—United States 2002. *Morbidity and Mortality Weekly Report.* www.cdc.gov/mmwr/preview/mmwrhtml/mm5233a1.htm.

Corbin, C.B., & Lindsey, R. (2007). *Fitness for life* (5th ed.). Champaign, IL: Human Kinetics.

Danielson, C. (1996). *Enhancing professional practice: A framework for teaching.* Alexandria, VA: Association for Supervision and Curriculum Development.

Federal Register, August 23, 1977, PL 94-142, *The Education for All Handicapped Children Act.*

Federal Register. (1990). *Individuals with Disabilities Education Act.* IDEA, 1997, [34 C.F.R. § 300.7©)+].

Gallahue, D.L. (1989). *Understanding motor development in children* (2nd ed.). Indianapolis: Benchmark.

Graham, G. (Ed.). (1992). Developmentally appropriate physical education for children. *Journal of Physical Education, Recreation, & Dance, 63,* 29-60.

Graham, G. (2001). *Teaching children physical education: Becoming a master teacher* (2nd ed.). Champaign, IL: Human Kinetics.

Hellison, D. (1985). *Goals and strategies for teaching physical education.* Champaign, IL: Human Kinetics.

Hopple, C. J. (1995). *Teaching for outcomes in elementary physical education: A guide for curriculum and assessment.* Champaign, IL: Human Kinetics.

Horvat, M., Block, M E., & Kelly, L.E. (2007). Developmental and adapted physical activity assessment. Champaign, IL: Human Kinetics.

Howley, E.T., & Franks, B.D. (2007). *Fitness professionals handbook* (5th ed.). Champaign, IL: Human Kinetics.

Kelly, L. E. (1987). Computer assisted instruction: Applications for physical education. *Journal of Physical Education, Recreation & Dance, 58,* 74-79.

Kelly, L.E. (1988). Curriculum design model: A university-public school model for designing a district-wide elementary physical education curriculum. *Journal of Physical Education, Recreation & Dance, 59,* 26-32.

Kelly, L.E., & Melograno, V.J. (2004). *Developing the physical education curriculum: An achievement-based approach.* Champaign, IL: Human Kinetics.

Knudson, D.V., & Morrison, C.S. (2002). *Qualitative analysis of human movement* (2nd ed.). Champaign, IL: Human Kinetics.

Kreighbaum, E., & Barthels, K.M. (1981). *Biomechanics: A qualitative approach for studying human movement* (2nd ed.). Minneapolis: Burgess.

Lavay, B., French, R., & Henderson, H. (2006). *Positive behavior management in physical activity settings* (2nd ed.). Champaign, IL: Human Kinetics.

Le Fevre, D.N. (2002). *Best new games.* Champaign, IL: Human Kinetics.

Marzano, R.J. (2000). *Transforming classroom grading.* Alexandria, VA: ASCD.

McGinnis, P.M. (2005). *Biomechanics of sport and exercise* (2nd ed.). Champaign, IL: Human Kinetics.

Melograno, V.J. (1984). The balanced curriculum: Where is it? What is it? *Journal of Physical Education, Recreation & Dance, 55,* 21-24, 52.

Melograno, V.J. (1996). *Designing the physical education curriculum* (3rd ed.). Champaign, IL: Human Kinetics.

Melograno, V.J. (1997). Integrating assessment into physical education teaching. *Journal of Physical Education, Recreation & Dance, 68,* 34-37.

Mohnsen, B.S. (2001). *Using technology in physical education* (3rd ed.). Cerritos, CA: Bonnie's Fitware.

Morris, G.S.D., & Stiehl, J. (1989). *Changing kids' games.* Champaign, IL: Human Kinetics.

Mosston, M., & Ashworth, S. (2002). *Teaching physical education* (5th ed.). San Francisco: Benjamin Cummings.

National Association for Sport and Physical Education. (2008). *PE-Metrics: Assessing the National Standards.* Reston, VA: Author.

National Association for Sport and Physical Education. (2002). *2001 Shape of the nation report.* Reston, VA: Author.

National Board for Professional Teaching Standards. (1994). *What teachers should know and be able to do.* Southfield, MI: Author.

National Commission on Excellence in Education. (1983). *A nation at risk: The imperative of educational reform.* Washington, DC: U.S. Government Printing Office.

National Commission on Teaching & America's Future. (1996). *What matters most: Teaching for America's future (summary report).* Woodbridge, VA: Author.

No Child Left Behind Act. (2001). Public law print of PL 107-110. U.S. Department of Education: Author.

Orlick, T. (1982). *The second cooperative sports and games book.* New York: Pantheon.

Pangrazi, R.P. (2004). *Dynamic physical education for elementary school children.* (14th ed.). San Francisco: Pearson.

Popham, W.J. (2001). The truth about testing: An educator's call for action. Alexandria, VA: ASCD.

Reeves, D.B. (2004). *Accountability for learning.* Alexandria, VA: ASCD.

Rink, J., Dotson, C., Franck, M., Hensley, L., Holt Hale, S., Lund, J., Payne, G., & Wood, T. (1995). *National standards for physical education: A guide to content and assessment.* St. Louis: Mosby.

Schmoker, M.J. (2006). *Results now: How we can achieve unprecedented improvement in teaching and learning.* Alexandria, VA: ASCD.

Sherrill, C. (2004). *Adapted physical activity, recreation, and sport: Crossdisciplinary and lifespan* (6th ed.). Dubuque, IA: McGraw-Hill.

Siedentop, D., & Tannehill, D. (2000). *Developing teaching skills in physical education.* (3rd ed.). Mountain View, CA: Mayfield.

Siedentop, D.J., Herowitz, J., & Rink, J. (1984). *Elementary physical education methods.* Englewood Cliffs, NJ: Prentice Hall.

Stonge, J.H. (2002). *Qualities of effective teachers.* Alexandria, VA: ASCD.

Swain, D.P., & Leutholtz, B.C. (2007). *Exercise prescription: A case study approach to the ACSM guidelines* (2nd ed.). Champaign, IL: Human Kinetics.

Ulrich, D.A. (2000). *The Test of Gross Motor Development-2.* Austin, TX: Pro-Ed.

U.S. Department of Education. (1991). *America 2000: An education strategy.* Washington, DC: Author.

U.S. Department of Health and Human Services. (1996). *Physical activity and health: A report of the Surgeon General.* Atlanta, GA: Author.

Walkley, J., & Kelly, L.E. (1990). The effectiveness of an interactive videodisc qualitative assessment training program. *Research Quarterly for Exercise and Sport, 60,* 280-285.

Wessel, J.A. (1976). *I CAN primary skills.* Austin, TX: Pro-Ed.

Wessel, J.A., & Kelly, L. (1986). *Achievement-based curriculum development in physical education.* Philadelphia: Lea & Febiger.

Wessel, J.A., & Zittel, L.L. (1995). *Smart start: Preschool movement curriculum for children of all abilities.* Austin, TX: Pro-Ed.

Wessel, J.A., & Zittel, L.L. (1998). *I CAN primary skills: K-3* (2nd ed.). Austin, TX: Pro-Ed.

About the Authors

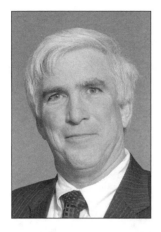

Luke E. Kelly, PhD, is a professor of kinesiology at the University of Virginia in Charlottesville. He has 30 years of experience working with public schools on evaluating and revising their general physical education curricula to meet the needs of students with disabilities. He has written six books and numerous articles on topics related to training general physical educators. He also has developed and validated a Web-based motor skill assessment program that allows teachers to assess students' motor skills.

Janet Wessel, PhD, is professor emeritus from Michigan State University. She has numerous publications in adapted physical education and has designed instructional systems and curricula for children with special needs. She has also presented I Can workshops and has developed and adapted program content, instructional design, and other activities relevant to cultural and educational settings. Dr. Wessel has received numerous awards over the years, including the Crystal Apple Honor Award in recognition of exceptional educators from the Michigan State University College of Education.

Gail M. Dummer, PhD, is a just-retired kinesiology professor from Michigan State University. For the past 30 years, she has taught university-level courses, conducted outreach projects, and conducted research related to adapted physical activity. She served as the director of the Michigan State University Sports Skills Program, in which university students provide instruction and coaching in sports skills to people with disabilities. She has received numerous awards over the years, including the 2008 Professional Recognition Award from the Adapted Physical Activity Council of AAHPERD.

Tom Sampson, PhD, is an assistant professor and chair of the education department at Olivet College in Olivet, Michigan. He is a former elementary physical education and adapted physical education teacher, and he has experience in implementing objective-based, outcome-driven curricula. He has also acted as a K-12 health and physical education curriculum coordinator and has been a field test teacher for the federally funded I Can adapted PE program.

You'll find other outstanding physical education resources at
www.HumanKinetics.com